ML

Who Touches This

Who Touches This

Selected Poems 1951-1979

Robert Hazel

The Countryman Press

TAFTSVILLE · VERMONT 05073

Some of these poems originally appeared in the following books
and periodicals:
Peoms 1951-1961, Morehead State University Press, 1961
American Elegies, North Dakota State University Press, 1968
American Poetry Review
Choice
Equal Time
Esquire
Southern Poetry Review

Library of Congress Cataloging in Publication Data

Hazel. Robert.
  Who touches this.

  I. Title.
PS3515.A9795W48   811'.54   80-10767
ISBN 0-914378-57-0
ISBN 0-914378-56-2 pbk.

Antonia Squitieri

1951-1971

Passing. One. We are passing. Two. From sleep we are passing. Three. Into the wikeawades warld from sleep we are passing. Four. Come, hours, be ours!

But still. Ah diar, ah diar! And stay.

—*Finnegans Wake*

CONTENTS

NYC

There now is your insular city. . . commerce surrounds it
with her surf. . . look at the crowds of water-gazers there.
                                                    —*Melville*

1.
Gray to the marrow, pale as tall smoke
across the East River
the boneyard of Queens burns

Into my window charred letters fall
from the grim incinerators,
some still legible, with lovers' initials

and the brown reek of fire

2.
Pools of blue children under the haze
under the sailing hats of nuns

3.
Private darkness strays into rubble
where the Catholic god and the Jewish god
grow weak stems in cinders

Terror is private
A woman is murdered in 38 windows

Everybody is nobody's keeper
Ask mercy of stray cats

The dim roar of traffic over bridged boroughs
comes savage and sad

4.
On an island staked out by stolen car aerials
professional liars in glass canyons cross
Madison Avenue and disappear
in secret Connecticut

Marcantonio's city of shattered wine bottles
and brown cut flesh rings Columbia in

In the midnight streets I hear
young whores cursing

5.
The smiling girl who committed suicide,
mistress of gem thieves, hid a black eye
under polaroid glasses

She screamed the length of her lover's coffin
She rode in a Cadillac long as a whore's dream

Lover, tell me the best hate
Murderer, tell me the best love

6.
The cold wind shines

A train clicks quietly under the iron grating
where, with axle-grease on a lead sinker,
a coatless man fishes for lost coins

I watch raw-knuckled care for all trivial, all small
And here

7.
Banks whisper money
Male whores reply
Oiled locks slide free

8.
Aluminum trucks bleat like lambs
hauling barrels, crates over the cobbles
Streets grow long with vegetables and messengers

Near dawn I walk among fishnets and boatloads of coffins

And where the streets move, treeless,
I hear pawnshop trumpets

9.
The ferry rides under gulls crying
in high monotones the water's given names
over Crane's forgotten bones

And wrecks passed without sound of bells

Acropolis builders, stand with me here, see how you failed!

QUEENS PLAZA

to CFB

And yet, suppose some evening I forgot
the fare and transfer...

—*Crane*

1.
The small trees in Queens
on the way to the neighborhood
church where the ikons
of Christ are painted red,
grow in small round plots
in fields of cement;

I saw a thin girl
at a bank of white candles
whose flames were the leaves
of her burnt childhood
and their smoke was the scented
cry of her dreams
in a chapel of plaster hands;

as we went to my place
in Brooklyn Heights
she talked about her dead father
and her mother, living alone,
in a brick apartment building
with five roofs over her head;

when fog closed down
the harbor and Brooklyn
near dawn I listened
to the foghorns while she slept,
then quickly her frightened eyes
strung on telephone wires
until she found me beside her;

to Chinatown and the Village,
we stood at the front window
of the train to see
the tracks curve down
into the 4th Street station,
and did not try to guess
which way the bending laughter
would run ahead, or confess
the terror running behind;

her face is clear always;
I love its shape; I see
her mouth move inaudibly
under mine with love.

2.
When the train screams
at the rails' flange
coming into Queens
under the neon signs
of Blackjack and Dentyne
chewing-gum, and the smell
of bakeries is strong,
I cannot remember
whether to change—change
for what station?
my mind cannot arrange
the free transfer;
change must be
only an illusion;

in March cold rain
falls in the city
and taxis make white
tracks from Manhattan
out to Queens, going
from the stone office buildings
to the brick apartments
where sycamores and umbrellas
shine in the neon

of bars and newsstands
with pieces of iron
laid on the wet papers
where the subways end
and the rain walkers
wiping their glasses
enter and exit,
their raincoats dripping
on the platforms
where we stood in the cold
many times together
waiting for a train.

COW SALT

for Henry Birnbaum

White the blocks stacked on the street
before a hardware store in Indiana, savory in the sun
Henry Birnbaum, *schön* as his peartree name,
asked what. I said, Cow salt.
He gave a New York weary shrug.
Cow salt? There's no such thing!

I bent & cradled the life-giver for
how many years of fertility—
O my rush deep into the green where
I set the salt!

I don't go anymore where it is hauled
stay miles & miles away from slaughter
It stalks me in dreams
Nor have I lately strolled on Avenue C
in New York City where Henry led   I fear
that little start to die

May I sit in your house, Hersh ben Simon, & see
on TV the Washington Redskins?   And on
your walls all the books & paintings
Love is simple permission

Trailing no clouds of glory, we come. . .
our teachers dead: Whitehall & Cargill—
friends in the earth or rotting in silence
In this grim interim of breath
the beast-me whimpers, unslaked,
calling to an emotive runt
I have dragged experiences behind me
like a mean dog   It snaps
Surcharge on my spirit? Nobody here to pay
I'm not in society, but log hours haunted
in a womb of green ferns

I choose nothing   I'm untracked
Yet less love was laid on the line than mine
O I have been beautiful as October!
Who will pay the tax now on my blemishes?

And you, Henry, not your brain clean
as a nail nor often wisdom can
fence chaos at the border of your last haircut
Billy Kilmer could have told you better
or your father, mystic Simon, closing the Sabbath over
the East River
Reason?   Forget Spinoza & Kant
rare archaic intoxicant   How many sober mornings
have you died trying to imagine a prayer
you cannot utter?

White on the street, the blocks of your disbelief
Lot's wife looked back, too

If the salt shall lose its savor
who will remember the sting
to my cut hand, to your blind eye
the first pain of holy?

POET TO PAINTER

My poet! he said
Now he is dead

Arthur Sappé could see lyric color
in an eyesore

His first outdoor show
in the Village, watercolors hooked on a row

of black iron spikes
before Judson Church

We belittled the guys
who bought buckeyes

hardly noticed his rainbow labor, heart's own,
purchased none

Back to West 26th Street,
the old slum, the reeking night

Five flights up from the garbage can
I followed soft inspiration

To the surf off Staten Island
with a saw & a gallon of wine

to cut driftwood for sculptures, grain
to hack, polish & form

Now hand melted, heart burned
& ashes thrown

9

on the gull-slanted domain
of Hart Crane's Brooklyn

water. Artist, I send
my death-greeting past that bend

where wounded men share
duty to quality in a mock civilization

purblind to rare vision
That beauty may wear
the brightness of despair

LETTER FROM THE LOVED WOMAN OF AVENUE A

Please defrost the refrigerator
Please water the plants with tepid water
The violets should be watered from the bottom lips
    of their dishes up
Eat the bacon and eggs   I even bought you grits
    second shelf
Get much work done

I love you and will see you at the AMTRAK

The sick nightmare jive you suffered through with me
    our first year when I was a "talky" girl!
Oh, but I feel so grown up now and send to you
    all my collective loves

I spent you blind, Baby, $2.35 for a catfish dinner
    in a little hole in the wall in South Carolina
In between alka seltzers I looked—like you told me—
    at the sluggish brown rivers and green pines
    and watched my reflection in the motel windows
    all very tricky because so crowded with despair

Along the railway from Richmond to Danville
    there's a stretch—is that the word?—
    of land, well wooded and hilly
    for you to look into and possibly buy
    to build our house on
    corn and beans for you, an herb garden for me
    and I promise not to burn the house down
    like your apartment on Sullivan Street that night

Please remember the train is due at 6:50 p.m.
Please know that I understand another kind of fire
    in my belly, the red coal of our child

TO A YOUNG WOMAN OF TWENTY
I CARRIED ON MY SHOULDERS AT FIVE

I was glad to see you
despite your Cowboy boots
Western jacket and hat
and your air of being interested
in nothing at all

Less glad to see your companions,
spineless young pups, trailing,
sniffing as if you were in heat,
not bold enough to mount you

I wish you more than young men
who think a well-spent night
is burning napkins in ashtrays,
who giggle, tote sleeping bags
not in Wyoming but Brooklyn
and cultivate holes in their socks

It's probably lucky for both of us
that I had no chance to speak
with you privately because
I might have said, "Timothy Leary
loves Doris Day" and you would
have had to run me through
with your Army Surplus bayonet

ODE TO THE TEENIES OF TOMPKINS SQUARE

Hissing agony to psychiatrists
girls without earth for their feet
women, ungreen, with hard knees
posters of Spain on their walls
hands unopened to live flowers
compulsively closed on men's cocks—
they pump out the male stream briefly
and lie down, sad and unwanted
grit in their angry eyes
fixed on their own crucifixions
no prayers in their dirty shawls

Girls in their New York uniforms
male from the crotch down
in their Lees and Levis
manly buckles and high boots
female from navel up
long hair, Peruvian blouses

Girls eating 40¢ pizza
their vinegar-stung cunts
dreaming of penetration
the gaumed girls of dough and cheese
hopeful wistful and snarling
blowing their brains out in brick cells
to the whisper of roaches
and the odor of marijuana

Russian and Roman fathers
teach reverence for the liferoot
how to fondle caress and jack it
suck power and swallow the magic
Some like to go down for kicks
their vaginas and colons so shot full
that only their mouths remain hungry

Nailed to the cold green benches
hurt-hearted girls spitting semen
huddled in the radiance
of psycho secret loneliness
their chorused clitori ringing
like tiny altar bells

WHO TOUCHES THIS

to Walter Freeman

Every time I dream, I am alive
Every time I remember a dream,
I know I have lived

                        ***

Mother, lie
Father, rise

                        ***

I live in the mountains and work the farm
my father and I cleared and kept green
I hear a creek bubble loud like my heart
and thrushes' wings whisper over the hill
I meet my boyhood on a gravel road
and see how beautiful I was then
honey Robert me

                        ***

Dreams! My skull explodes with dreams
like the white heads of dandelions
I sit in a room in Manhattan
hearing empty bottles fall,

                        ***

savage words in other windows,
the gears of a garbage truck
I live in the pain of my father
who tried to cross his hands
when he choked and choked
when the last stroke struck

                        ***

If I have no way to go
that way is good
I am learning how not to live
I shall forget every valuable thing
last and first forget the woman
I said love to said love said love

***

I will tell you a bitter thing, blind heart:
the wild ways you have perfected
the way hunters create the life of a deer with knives

***

The purpose of learning is to forget before you die
But a man must try to learn something unspeakable,
    something that makes him tremble

***

The lone black man
in this gritty precinct
of flower children
woke me at 4:00 this morning
crying, "Whore of Babylon!"
Near sleep I heard something
perfect as a dream
so certain that I felt
it would survive my waking
It was only the hoarse
repetitions of a drunk man
shouting, cursing, weeping
how this nation was killing

all his innocent children
Yet strangely when he stood
pounding the garbage cans
and imploring, "America!"
the word sounded beautiful
as if he believed it

***

I have become my face
My face smiles for me
on public occasions
when a man's peers
are all photographers
Then at 5:00 p.m.
I return to an old vacancy
called my heart
And where will you speak, Robert,
after 5:00 p.m., and to whom?
Tell a dimestore mirror
how you have loved
father & mother, brothers & sister
and a woman from Brooklyn?
God, drag these loves
at the end of a leather halter
like the dead cats and dogs
I dangled as a child
at the end of a dusty rope
before they begin to stink!

***

I have written this in a ring-binder
that belonged to a friend who cut his wrists
There is a smear of blood on the cover

***

It is nearing dawn
This is the way I say no to God
and the way God laughs back at me
in the cold shirt of my skin

INDIANA

North from Louisville

The window blind is brown
in my window night
falls from a tower
holding a clock
across the river a city
glows, and beyond
fields of winter wheat
church spires and silos
bodies measure shadows
no words are heard

the rented room is quiet
the pingpong game in the hall
stopped at eleven
the pale girls have gone
to the White Castle
here silence is like
Dreiser dead, with a landlady
bent over his corpse
while her radio plays "Stardust"

I never draw the blind
whenever light comes
I do not want to miss it
light is my profession
it accustoms me to nights
when rats chew orange peels
in the wastecan near my desk,
and I stand at the window
where smoke from the flues
settles blue on the pane

the bridge looks handwritten
I draw my initials
the way you trace your identity
when you are not thinking
where my hand has rubbed,
light, not my name, comes through.

Harrodsburg: The Cemetery

The highway runs ahead of my injured eyes,
seeing only the concupiscent angels frozen:
the intuitive shame of motionless things,
the absence of consciousness and memory
    in the permanent grin
praise comes without honor, death without dignity;
the finite insult of prayers
takes no account of the distances
a live hand tapped electrically
in a red brick station against a green hill

an ingenuous painting might show a steam engine
    and gondolas paralleling a river
as on a pingpong table in a basement
a group of women suggests patience
while town clocks measure the distances
from railyard to courthouse to coal-bucketed kitchens

but nowhere is the recognition that love or grief
    can be real.

Indianapolis

The policeman's whistle is clear and thin
at the white island of monuments on Meridian
Street, weighted with tableaus of frontiersmen:
Clark in green bronze, sword drawn,
leans towards Vincennes, and pale green
water booms from the fountain
and settles to a stillness under the reign
of blue-and-gold State banners on aluminum

poles that face the tarnished Capitol dome
above six Corinthian pillars; the limestone
wilderness stretches, treeless, to the open
arcade of the bus terminal, a slam
of light down Market Street to the Harrison
Hotel, under a long red-and-white sign

gamblers with dry faces and sallow skin
ravel in the weaving walk of equal blacks with brown
expectations; the Circle Theater kills time
with a film based on a Lloyd C. Douglas novel shown
in technicolor; and under his white helmet a modern
gladiator from North Vernon
creates Speed, a flying
red horse stenciled on the blue racer's engine,
while at the roller rink caryatids in
flesh-colored stockings support the roof, go nowhere in a din
of lucky wheels; on stage at the burlesque, near the wing
an Irish boy sings "Mandalay"; a bronze woman
with torch, on the monument's peak, faces south down Meridian.

Bloomington

The same way prayers end,
letters always begin:

Dear Myself,
                              Today
I heard music, drowned
in sunlight and slaughterhouse blood
and a strange sense of rubber
tires rolling around
the speedway without cars
or drivers, because tonight
after Hoagy Carmichael went back
to the piano in the gym
and Wendell Willkie returned
to the Law library

20

my father called me in
from a war to put on the earphones
and listen to Berlin
I had to listen then
because tomorrow everybody
would be in our attic,
my father's workshop,
to listen to the first
short-wave receiver in town
and hear the romantic music
of central Europe as if
it were one inch away
in Berlin a band was playing
from under the workbench
the color-coded wires
sped into the world.

Milan

In the darkened houses
they watch television
Their walls are scrolled
with Christian mottoes in red wool

Coal piles by the railway
are dense and odorless

The county held the world's record
for corn yield per acre

Mechanical cornpickers stand like giraffes
Sheep make few night noises

Clocks are meaningless

Before a train arrives the switchblock
obeys a steel instinct for direction

No lives are suddenly sidetracked
Loss is criminal

21

A black standpipe wears
orange letters: STATE CHAMPS, 1954

Young cars ease to macadam
and accelerate with sexual squeals

The green glass of bottles
broken in the street

looks American

When Dreiser wrote he had no readers
When Willkie ran he got few votes

My cousin in bluejeans wept for Dean
and raced her Chevy the wrong way

down all the one-way streets
in search of ice cream

I did not suggest she go to a doctor
Who is insane?

Labels are dead wonders

Who is free? I had a gray jacket
too tight across the back

I strained against force,
my life confronted by perfect deadness

as I lifted the canvas mailbags
with brass padlocks, thrown from trains

I like to stand in the icy cones
of trains diminishing towards morning

It is not yet dawn
There is not enough light.

MONUMENT CIRCLE

for Lannis Thrasher

In cement leaves, with pigeons and rustling girls, the carved
                                        figures rumor
    deaf close histories;
this symmetry of white is your boyish hunger among cigar bands,
    wine bottles and bare-headed warriors;
red, the instant affinity of my blood, dear cousin, for yours,
take as the first knowledge of what we are and sweetly ever were;
accept black, our tattered lingo for the long ambulance
that draws you, drugged, south from Indianapolis—
the wooden-spoked Buick you drove past Monument Circle to arrive
    at the hollow points of steel needles
doesn't count for much on a used car lot; the hypodermics taste
    the new sugar and the undried blood;
the final sweetness becomes as in photographs: all untearful
blasphemies whispered to sober daughter-wives standing
    awkwardly in the lobby of the veterans' hospital;

these figures, quiet in the fountain's rain,
this pride of monuments pities our limestone;
these stones at the meridian of our earth close us among
girls we were photographed with—a rural joke, this grinning
arm-linked stand with strangers, in our pockets the contraband
    of crimped bottle tops, sailors' caps, and the white husks
        of our pigpens;
the frozen pumps and empty buckets
are only relics of our inaudible childhood:
you with your black hat, baggy suit and determined scowl,
your tobacco-stained hands holding the trivial
    histories of Terre Haute and Evansville;

23

who, in my nightdreams, is as deprived as you?
who stands unslaked where the water shoots out from the fountain
    at the center of our dead city
over the graceless effigies of Union volunteers, where tongues
    of water
spew and curve down their glittering acclaims to your dry pity,
as in my nightmares, you?
forgive my staring at you unaware, my terror
of the photograph shot beside the polished car, the black door
    you will abruptly enter;

in Monument Circle at night cornet and tambourine play;
you have left me under the weight of charitable coins, so heavy!
how can I, in your absence,
hear them sing, and see
the white faces of secret girls and the stone lunge of history across
    their knees, the broken columns,
without remembering your noon grin, its dimestore permanence?

there you are with your smile, clear body;
there you are with your invisible landscapes
    rolled under night;
you illumine with your silence and star-faced curiosity
the heavy slaughterhouses south of the reeking city;
you clarify for an instant the tumult of switch-engines
    at crossings,
tall boys running in gymnasiums, and the capture of girls;
between the quiet paralysis of statuary and the quick thirst of stone
you retrace our country
where the blue windows of stonemills shine through black thickets
    and sudden patches of snow;

I am surprised by a green gourd's ripening
though I recall our overweening gardens, the heavy berries;
I remain alive to pantomime your dawns
over ration cans and toxic sleeps,

the earth binding you;
I crave deep minerals, living always, and the bright increment
    of furrows that curl my ankles;
I want the life that gave me this holy flesh, this form, this keen
    plow to carve out brisk sunflowers and onions,
this torment;

O the fruit breaks our speckled trees down!
and time's brown scrawl on the fields sure of weeds' fast colors
                                                    in fall
traces winter to window;
I want the life of your hand-me-down flesh
before the boy stirs at last
the deepest of all vegetal memories
and the bayonet follows his entreating wounds;

slow tides of brown blood barter existence for forgetting;
I invent the long days of our curious and questing indolence;
people stream about me in little black cars;
military caps sail brightly away;
on this holiday of my words and my dreaming
the tones of many voices on forgetful porches,
and leaves, brown and pious, affront your quiet acre
where wreaths of wired flowers stare
and crossed rifles shoot briefly;

concerning the slow echoes, the warm grass with its yellow
    worn distances—these turn
by the endless car windows to a perfect horizon,
and in the spade-gashed abyss between being and forgetting
the grave discovers what has been given to it;
you lie whole; wounds heal, fastenings roll from you.

HILL ABOVE BEDFORD

Carved stones legend us human and dwarfed on this hill
where the serious dead, divine in their ugliness, lie;
snail-horned stones drink the rain quietly,
and we who have felt the thirst of minerals and the hunger
    of animals at dusk
resign ourselves to contemplation of the holy perfection
    of ugliness;

what is beautiful is completely human,
and a stone is not a thing to plant
unless hard wishes have worn away
and nothing is left but love;

our fathers' land is poor, the timber second-growth;
all their tall illusions are cut down;
their walls are broken by cries of foxes and crickets;
and we who cannot build because we must sing in summer,
our minds made intricate by the sickness of music,
have these stones to stare down vanity;

here moments cannot stay, but fall trophies away
    like the wings of dinosaurs;
we cannot enter these stones, placed at the center
    of chance and innocence,
only a white monotone of instants that belong
    to life, and its quick going;
dressed fit to kill, we walk on this hill,
    Cain among the gravestones;
here pain moves leisurely, and cannot be put by;

serene in their ugliness, our fathers' uncharmed clocks,
with precise indifference to our humanity, are silent;
dressed in black cloth, satin round the arm,
we walk all afternoon, lame and beautiful,
knowing these bones and flowers we carry perish
    and shall not come again;

in a cedar tree, chants of young doves resume
    as we pass;
the fence rails are black, the burdocks green
under the blowing rain of spring; we listen.

CATAFALQUE

As I grow young and new
I forget sound and light,
radios and rainbows
traffic lights bend
over streets in rain,
the loud drop of tinfoil
on plazas in New York,
the hail of weed seed
on sod in Indiana.

I grow new into silence.
I keep only the deaf,
hanged by white wires
that run to invisible ears,
the crippled with candle legs
in the sanctuary of steel braces,
priests in brown robes,
sandaled in snow,
rabbis in white stockings
closing the Sabbath
across tin cans and cyclone fences,
arms held like broken wings.

I hold deafness and blindness.
I lead myself
into new silence.
For the first time I see
my young wife's face,
the silent symmetry
of her blind eyes.
I have never seen
even in an apple
or a cadaver
so much beauty.

New things grow as I grow
and fall into silence.
I do not know anything
except dictionaries and catalogues
I read as a boy
in my sheepskin coat,
barricaded with rifles
in my green and cindery country,
in cornfields and steeltowns
dressed up with people
who were all beautiful.

I keep the deaf
trapper of foxes
whose dumb hands
flew away at dusk,
and the girl who never
saw a mirror.

This is my nature;
to guess stones and flowers
before they rot and seed
the wind its random motion.

I cannot remember
when I grew young and younger.
When I was twelve, my father
gave me a dictionary
so I would know
what I mean.
I will never know.
To know would be unlike me.
To inherit blindness and deafness
I teach myself.

I keep for fields and cities
a plain map that I drew
from memory in grammar school,
with mountains in brown,
lowlands in green.

My geography is simple.
I lead myself here
by a red wrist
into the captivity
of bright October sun.

In my new greed,
I lead myself to the stone
steps of a gray building
under the clock tower
of a university.

Beside this temporary scaffold
of books, maps, leaves,
boys and girls pass,
carrying books and candy.
I have never seen
even in broken bottles
and varnished crutches
so much beauty
as their quick legs and skulls.

This is the braille
of my lost vision.   My country
is raised and shallow.   My country
is red and yellow.   I wear
its coat of many-colored lies.
In my hands, without fingerprints,
I keep this dust to quicken
a new death.
                                        Bells strike
over New York and Indiana,
an hour wide.   Hearing the time
announced in bronze,
I go past a hardware store
with white blocks of salt
out front.   I go, among students,
carrying each other's hands,
without a word, and blind.

SILENCES

Childhood

I heard corn grow
I dented the moon with an air rifle

Nobody else in Indiana could do that!

My parents' god demanded suffering
Should I have tried another way?

An American child, I played a radio
so I'd not have to listen to music

Musicians don't understand silence

Magic is silence
silence smells like new shoes

Ancestry

Inheritor of Whitman, Hopkins, Crane
trousers, belt, shirt, socks & moonburn

Philosophy

Charles Dickens & James Wright excuse our crimes
Ivan Karamasov & I will never forgive us

Simone Weil said it: Humanity is one
of God's least successful experiments

I have friends whose stomachs are cut.
They are silent as sea turtles

If water will fall, let it
Water gives you no choice but silence

The Condition of the Culture

Intelligent conversation is lacking because
few understand the intricacies of football

Hamlet as quarterback & Ophelia as wide receiver
draws a blank at Radcliffe

But Shakespeare knew Columbus, Ohio
His mind was cleansed by that high terror

In New York City roaches picked
my teeth clean while I slept

Poverty

Good women stewed the broth of my troubles

What troubles?
I am only dying

In return I gave them all my money
They held me closest just before leaving

Ambition

To ride in triumph through Indianapolis
Unveil my limestone statue on Meridian!

Reply to Ambition

My favorite aunt: What *ever* will become of you!
Her favorite nephew: Nothing

Croquet

They're about to stake out
and I don't even have a position

Isolation

Other people do things
Why does nobody invite me?

What was love like?
The echo of minnows?

Goodbye, Poem

Why hang you on the line to dry?
I lick glue
It is the hoof of a dead horse

WASHINGTON

Arlington Cemetery

So it may be clear and inconceivable
as murders augured in childhood's long evils
and be seen burning down cities over popcorn
    and police whistles

let it appear heavy at the bottom, stable
as women leaning to Lincoln's or Lenin's face,
wishing their sons not alive to create again
    Shiloh or Budapest,
only their own radiant intrusion among rifles

and blue as poultry hung in shop windows
imitating abundance, clear but inconceivable,
as meat cannot appear in the public imagination
    clucking or grazing
but only takes shape in the controlled light
    of ovens

as the women cannot imagine pain until it
    suddenly is

then blindly in a thicket of elbows and knees
    seeming to grow, though broken,
let it be detailed as fingerprints, firingpins
and the green patinas of bronze idols;
let it wear thorns;

a marble sarcophagus chiseled of time
used as a watering trough by an Italian farmer
makes a museum of the mind
but if an American wished to be buried in a Cadillac
that would let it be even clearer
and less conceivable;
Sunday drivers are mystified by head-on collisions
     that condense time,
and the rituals of ambulances;
history becomes a pattern of clean-shaved euphemisms:

French immigrants who manufacture gunpowder
     are sanctified by Jefferson;
young gangsters love and respect their parish priests;
all is safe; all like *Life* is true;

then let it pry jewels from altars
to ornament the bridles of palominos;
let it come down from effigies with ivory faces
and its blood disappear quickly from windshields;
let it turn wine into water.

To the Constituents of the Congress

> *"... they are always guiltless... innocence is a kind
> of insanity..."*—Graham Greene

I was your honey and ash,
taught to prefer mattocks to mathematics;
I went to a state university
where mentally crippled children came, unable
to think, hardly able to feel, asking
     to be rescued;
your bewilderment was my confusion;

in this there is no stopping;

matters were settled; unlikely gods alone
    are strong and good;
real men are weak and sinful;
and you who inherited the fabled Christ
    of mirage-following nomads

find in this there is no back-tracking;

theocrats and humanists called their country
out of a dying world to create new innocence—
"The Americans who instituted the monkey trial
    in Dayton
have alone proved consistent," Freud said;

convinced of your innocence, you
hear your allies accuse you
of vices invented by your enemies;

the liberated prove ungrateful
for their liberation,
the reconstructed
for their reconstruction;
the colonial peoples resent you;
driven by these provocations, you
plan to exert your power
to compel history
to conform to your illusions;

in this there is no relenting;

I was your violation,
your money and trash,
bought with Bibles and athletics,
taught to distrust poets and mathematicians;

in this there is no loving;

and unless you know that Jefferson was the first
and Forrestal the last American hero—
and understand the awful transition—
you cannot even know what questions to ask
    to clarify you;

in this there is no wisdom.

Georgetown

May it please our unlikely saviours from the moment
    of their squandering blood
that we quietly here in Washington
listen at night to our friend, a Roman
by birth and faith, read Dante in the Italian;

may our pleasure seem innocent
    as thorns or a brood
of thieves breaking up before the sun
deafens a clear cruel bird, and tedium
clanks a veil of vending machines in the Pentagon;

earlier we had experienced a torment
    of Etruscan horses, loud
on Constitution Avenue, stone mane
breaking on necks torqued wildly, an intuition
of Marini's to unbridle time in the museum;

afterwards we passed a tamed cement
    percheron that stood
outside the Labor Department, in its line
nothing of running, and remembered the pain
of Pound at St. Elizabeth's and Perse in the Wardman;

and thought of Forrestal's flight from the ardent
    window to the sod
at Bethesda while the airport vane
cried clear weather east to the aluminum
bird, a wreath of brains rustling in its design.

37

Statuary Hall

The dancers, candled in their flames
cold on eyes and brittle hair,
cold on their marble shoulders, light
that is not pleasure but a way
to know by limits, and they know
time by decorum and love by art,
they find this way to imitate
the never final partially true—
they pray with dancing if they pray—
before the movement as they move
subsides to consciousness, before
the movement pauses as they take
this partial truth of movement and
believe pure energy is true
as if dead men were surely dead
because they move so little, as though
the deadness of ideas and men
is always carried slowly and
is true because this movement holds
the shaping deadness finally in;
they know that chaos, if they fail,
becomes a city, and if they move
falsely then all their partial truths
become a stammering of blood;
they move with courage, perilously
in plights of incense as they breathe
freedoms tallowing coldly out.

STAR

for Frederic Thursz

All day, higher than the heads of executioners,
the earth rose against the clean blades of bulldozers
and fell without echo at dusk on galaxies of bones:
the seedless bodies of bearded men, milkless women,
children with dark stars sewn on remnant clothing;
in the leaf-green country surrounding Dachau the discoverers
climbed down from the iron of their machines
and smoked on the raw mounds, mouth deep in bones.

> At the end of history
> these
> were discovered dead:
> a victory
> over starvelings whose knees
> bled;
> the beauty of the head
> and eyes
> of a fly or a Jew, something to be
> crushed and buried
> at the beginning of history.

On the iron crosses, on the claws of black eagles,
on the cold edges of the voices of young men,
on the shields of tanks and weapons carriers,
on the Bronze Age swastikas, on the tenons of oak tables
of knights in their tarnished lust married to violence,
on the Druid trees in wolf-toothed swamps, on wire cutters,
they were caught on the crosses, dismembered and killed.

> In the darkest nights stars grow.
> Black threatens them, always.
> Some are clotted with red.
> Some drift in the incandescence of the sky.
> Some are goblets lifted, held for a moment
> in a strange land.

YOUNG MEN, YOUNG WOMEN

for Nancy MacDonald

In these Christ-hurt born-damned days
to tell you my truth would be criminal, to say would be
first I love you as I hate myself for my false life
of tempered lies to your unhardened skulls, is
to walk away, after seeing you in sunlight, to my dark house
in these deaf and dumb days, and to tell you

No, it is not this
No, it is not that
No, it is not even the other
It is not May Day or Christmas or Passover
It is not like anything you have ever thought

It is not even grass near water near trees, and
is not the incredible skill of your knees and fingers, and
is not the timeless stare of your young clear eyes, and
it is not history or drama of Oedipus, Jesus or Lear, and
it is not rhythmic, as in making love, but

it is more like sickness, if you are alone, and
it is no honor, no honesty, and is
bad education, bad politics, bad art, and it is
the way a child is at birth and an old man at death, and

It is the face you see on my face

GUARD OF HONOR

in memory
John Fitzgerald Kennedy

West to Dallas

Leave the flattering libraries, the graceful Eastern towns
Leave the untold beads and the uncounted leaves of grass
Leave the blue panes of cathedrals, the red leather of law,
    the white silence of poetry
Take yourself to Texas in an open car
Be for one moment the advertised Zero of infantile people:
    rich boy in a big car, hair wild, teeth clean:
    young god without wound

West is the place to die It stands for death
No law except chance and impulse in that country:
    land blazing and sterile, cold with the howls
    of sun-crazed and moon-frozen animals
    with torn fur, then sun on the carcasses.
West is the place to die, my President

By day in a freeway
cavalcade of sunburnt limousines,
you ran the gauntlet of leather and lead
On the thin fabric of law between reason and chaos
you laid your head,
blood on the temple, then sound of a rifle
swaddled in oil
Hungry hands were waving
A black woman wept into her purse

Riderless Horse

From Andrews Field you ride into the Capital
A guard of honor escorts your sudden corpse
   down an aluminum ladder

Your widow stalks your body through an avenue
of bare sycamores, and one answering bell,
leading heads of state
   to altar and precipice

On the birthday of your son, your widow
walks bars of a dirge on the pavement
   towards fountain and abyss

Among swords of sunlight drawn by the spokes
   of the caisson
and the white manes of horses, she walks
   into noon and midnight

Above the muffled drums, the high voice
of a young soldier
tells the white horses how slow to go

before your widow and children, walking
behind the flag-anchored coffin—
and one riderless black horse dancing!

Widow

and so she took a ring from her finger
and placed it in his hands

Let her take his blood
   on her tongue,
his being wine
   at her green altar,
the sacrament of summer
   in her veins.
Heal her, her children
   with books and duties,
with winter land for walking,
   a child in her arms,
and no office
   except the natural care
of fall weeds bending,
   left, driven
And may she be
   fall, weeds, all
beauty's luck and fullness.
   Heal, make her well
with my country's bloom
   Let her have to know
   and not learn again

Supplication of the Poor

Bi-partisan committees of the Congress hail
   the hearse into Pennsylvania Avenue
Men in the Congress who were blinded by your vision
   and refused your living acts
pave the long route of your cortege
   with sanctimonious lies—
always the machinery for plunder and blood
   not yours then, or now—
the market rises and falls
Rich men pay no taxes
Lack-law rules
the substance is eaten
The husks drift in the wind
My President, where can we go?
Into what country
where the white-poor and the black-poor
do not have to barter dignity for bread?

The Post-Christian Era: An Oration

The witless prayers of children in the dark
   must ebb into silence
The eunuchs of Rome and New York
   must burn their robes
The violent and guilty boyhood of nations
   carrying rifles and crosses
must end and be forgotten

All the sacred emblems
   of religious awe, of tribal arrogance
   that have killed you
   must be laid down:
   the plowshares that were beaten into swords,
   the sacred wine-drops molded into bullets,
   the blinding cores of atoms
   that have killed you—
   all must be buried

The creation of gods to forgive
the evil in men,
the orgies of guilt and expiation,
must be left behind in the same way
men once shed the long hair from their bodies
and lost their fangs

Let them lay all their rings and weapons,
with their archaic beauty and terror,
on your grave

Light at Arlington

At Arlington the fall sunlight dies
Across the dark Potomac, Lincoln sits, hands on stone knees
At Arlington no steel or silver, no sword or chalice will remain
    clear as your eyes

President I love as my grandfather loved Lincoln,
in the silence after the bugle, lie down
Lie in your forest of stone
Lie close to Lincoln
On the dark hill a flower of light is blooming
    clear as your eyes were

CINDERS

to Wade Donahoe

". . . what business has the poor face of the man who officiates as poet? None but to disappear, to vanish and to become a pure nameless voice breathing into the air the words. . ."

—Ortega

Figure

to R.B.

The blue guard in the museum
stands quietly behind the crystal of his watch
I do not care what time of day it is   what day
but look past the back of a woman's head
into a triptych set against the wall's mosaic
the wings folded on brass hinges slightly
forward like a sleeping bird's

She is waiting for me to speak
but I do not know how any longer
I have forgot what vowels are so sacred
she must not hear them

I do not know any longer
whether the speaking would be
to the full face, or right or left profile
She might be the central point seized in some god's beak
or the parabola of all wing-deafened women

46

I do not even think any longer
what communication might be   I know only
that the young woman requires drama
two voices in monotonous strophe and antistrophe
two bodiless voices recalling dreamily
something performed in a place
of no dimensions   by persons without blood

Where the oblong medulla tapers
to a May Apple root coursing down her back
the vowels are only electricity   a pulsing
formless   secure   Nothing is going to happen
It is not as if I tossed pebbles at a lucid skull
high up where a light burns for my darkness
The head of the woman is turned away

I wish my voice may be lost finally
in her contemplation of sound
My voice must carry nothing to vary
the currents of her sentience
The speaking is only to beat pure oblivion
on her ear's three delicate bones

No place unwinds murmur and color
beasts listening   people walking about in clothing

To speak is to lean forward and enter emptiness.

Mirror

I have made something I will not remember
very long   I have made only this sign
These words that gesture to me are not important
I do not mean them   If I meant,
the words would seem to express things
that I am in continuous possession of
This is impossible to the mirrored world
Silvered and carboned, the mirror is cold and thin
Nothing it ever was stirs within it
Nothing is presented to it that was not otherwise
Glass is the will of fire, disinheriting all
the fire had signed and crossed with a leap

I do not want to say again
I have seen a world of wool and oboes
so long as the river runs softly against the shores
of my voice
or that it not wake the woman who sleeps there
This would be singing   But who would believe
desire can always mean singing?   My words say nothing

Rocks   wheels   idiots—
That there was no subject, ever
I did not care
at the time of seeing
when I thought the sand
is burning   the air is melting
and numberless gusts of fire
create the mirror: all knowledge, all being
That there is no subject   and finally
nothing has been said does not matter

48

I do not even know
how what is said differs from what goes unsaid
what orders of the flesh deployed in mirrors
have been surprised in attitudes of perfection
what oceans of sound crawl under the skin of silence
The world lies uncreated   The makers die
at some point near the beginning

I stand in the white halcyons of undiscovered worlds
whose creatures are too surprised to fly away
as in the sudden gaze of a mirror
one has no time to turn away
from the first image, the one always believed
Turning requires another surface
The silver dust of a mirror is thin and clear

One act is all one mirror can endure.

Nothing

In this first year of Nothing's being
the hour the iron clock strikes
and blue pigeons and tan pigeons
fan the air to flame
and return to jell on rotten cornices
separate   glowing with the anguish of distinctness
it seems that I should not have tried to join
unlike things
that relations which appear substantial are always false—
That the sun will rise tomorrow and end the sleep of lovers?
If I refuse to believe the sun will rise?—
Even if everything we wished were to happen
this would only be chance   random motion
purified of any meaning
For this reason
I do not make words I might have made
for a man and a woman

That would have been before the bathing of pure Absence
the nativity of Nothing
and its being wrapped in white cloth
before the pigeons lofted their loud grieving
when I might have made a harmony
of unlike things in the likeness of a word
of hard and durable alloy for the oneness
of a man and a woman

But it is not there when I speak
It is Nothing   That is only its name
This is not to know the thing but the name only
This is to know Nothing
This is to give myself away freely
and to represent my humanity
by a stage-direction
for which no play will be written

A world of the happy is another from a world of the unhappy
This is only to say death has always been
that death is not an event of life that changes
that death is not lived through
that death is not an experience

That in this death worlds do not change but end.

Drum

Have circuses for the living
and the dead who are so noticeably not moving
that you heap earth on   or burn
but have also a parade for the dead
who fill the tents and television rooms
or walk in plate-glass canyons
looking as if they were alive   Some of them
are at this moment applauding red-and-white clowns
Some are weighing their bodies on public scales
in which they drop a penny to see their good fortune
Others hold your face between their hands
and cast gregarious shadows
as they step through the heads of drums
and emerge in an arena of gold sawdust

If a group of people arrive talking and singing
have them step through the drum
The zebra deaths   accept them   Discover
that emotion is not obscene
even when completely surprised:
a frightened man is dying
with impatience to see if God is
A girl pulls long white days from a stem
counting: he loves me, he loves me not

Begin the parade with a herd of zebras
See the wayward whimsical gait
of creatures that go unshod   Remember
that the ultimate reality is a circle of animals
who do not live only to develop lines in their faces
Laughter is serious
                        If young men set fire
to the tent hasten them through the drum
to find themselves in the dressing room of the aerialist
where they can see her as she would be
splashed by a fireman's hose or dipped in a barrel
to see her clear thighs standing among reeds
far from the arena

If you will follow zebras with clowns
to go along the curb pinching the bright faces
of the dead   not incorruptible   then have
drums beat a measure for walking
the long walking in lines that lead nowhere
There is always a dream of perfect chaos
A dream of fire is what a circus is for
What else could so have lifted their faces
out of dreariness?   Recall
that among certain ancient peoples
it was believed if their minds were lost they were dead
though they laughed and ate and drank
and surely thought
the ash that bound their ecstasy was real

And when bodies at their lengths unfold in silence
if they are black from charring do not loathe them

Watch them   See how quick they change!

Alto

The man at the piano in Harlem
drinking a mixture of beer and white wine
is playing "After Hours" by Erskine Hawkins
and remembering the Deuces of New Orleans
A black river flows from Barbados
through the gullet of an alto man

So that nobody can look in
the windows are painted green
The rudimentary eyes of radios
are green and narrowed in the dark walls
under arbors of telegraph wires
while the eyes stare
and the time-signal chimes
in outlying centers of impulsive loss

The dying agitation of a pebble dropped in a pool

Such parliaments we hear in a back alley
Young lords with multiple tongues
clucking in subtle rapport
Behind green windows burgeoning of horns
in the register of noon
Through green windows they ride out in turn
Lords with reed-sweet mouths and crows' hands

The yolk of a bird's egg broken on his head
a naked child walks about a village
his steps uncertain, his balance precarious
walking a dusty road between mullein stalks
and cucumber vines   He hears
the bull-roarer, the sacred flutes
sees the masks and the magic ouangas

Sometimes the child sees a white face
that hangs for a moment like mistletoe
in halls of doubtful ancestry   Sometimes
walking in the sparrowed lane he gasps
at a white statue with outstretched hands
His mind richer in orchestration then
draws a purple skin over a green grape
that coasts the risen currents of summer
winey where the heat clings
to the undersides of leaves when the sun is softest

On the Gold Coast of Florida
the moon rides south to winter   and
round a coral hotel a frieze of persons
carved hastily, ill-shaped, gregarious
tell each other over cocktails
how Biscayne Bay glimmers in blind windows

entertain us   what if it's only smoke   only air?
that's for the time being   that too goes down
The lies blow trivial as the leaves of potted palms
entertain us   but that's for the time

Now it is after hours   In his mind
a clay road runs through South Carolina in August
after the cotton-picking
when fishermen doze at the creeks
and deep-bodied women in cabins
putter with beeswax, dried fruits, beans
The child recalls resinous cat-faces
slashed on the turpentine pines
He is afraid to take his lunch to school
Grease spots on the brown bag stare at him
He remembers a sweet-sour taste in his teeth
He pauses to adjust the reed of the saxophone
instrument of his birth delivered
with bloody cord still folded round him

entertain us   reach us
across rail yards and nightmares of ingots, Manhattan,
a violence unsubdued by music,
the tall gray island
reflecting the gasoline flares burning
in New Jersey
we will pay you

The men on drums and piano
wait for the alto man
The moon was yellow
The chanted *go* of voices
disturbs a school of minnows in his veins
Now his only thought is how high the moon is
above his ducktails preened with vaseline
and crossed where they tail off deep in the river marsh
He lies an inch above the water's skin
held by whole monotonies of tone
When he listens he hears always the same tone
Song of a redwinged bird in the audio
Now we have to go
Now we have to go.

SOUTH

to B.J. Parrott

1.
I see water walk
I see children fly
I hear men and women plot
flowers finite in the bloom
I hear them speak a room
into madness into night
I hear the sick and lame
recite their lips and arms against
empty windows broken panes

Bankers, doctors, money to you
Priests, lawyers, justice to you
But black hands still hands
still eyes black house, hear
I see your dirty smiles
tractors aprons caps furrows
your guitars and green whiskey
I see your pencil marks
on brown paper lumber walls
Steal, lic, grovel, fawn
Take any iron that lies loose
any woman any ladder
Grin the bars that jail you now
Common, Common, O my father!
Common girls in tall white heels
over roadhouse gravel, boys
in white coats with red flowers
withering on your lapels!

I hear the crossed priest pray
and the prosecutor sneer
and the banker count his liens
and the doctor wash his hands
of us over our live bodies
over our thin coats and shoes.

2.
White, quit chicken
Black, quit lard
Needles, quit cotton
Whores, quit street

The sun falls down
The trees lean down
The birds fly down
The faces look down
Shadows climb down
My father dies alone
My mother lies down
The fires die down
Their breath's bright crown
dies down like bloom
this spring like dawn
on time, all time
Love in its light down
comes to its brief claim

Men, quit work
Women, quit church
Let the vines run
in the garden
Let the trees grow Let the cold
Christ quit breathing twice

3.
Time stay love stay brain stay
I feel therefore I
stay where late we sing
We cause light to wheel day
heart-roar rib-silence
sun ice seed freeze
stolen fire early ash
We make injury pay the scar
I feel therefore am
flower post nail stone
I am love after love
I am buried without a harvest
due I am dying new
Brightness falls from the air
Girls have died drunk and young
O let the lamps burn
on tables bread wine music
Seed my brain into time
A growth of green ringed with hands
to protect your little veins
deep under the last freeze
Dust has closed your eye
I see therefore I
am sick and must die
Only lies are given me
Grass even lies to me
Earth tells me ripe lies
green against the fact of stone
Pity on us love in us terror in us
tears on us hands on us light in us
waste of us loss of us breath in us
pain in us growth of us light across us
Time's green last heard light.

4.
Timbers warp stones crack
Arms and hammers watch them fall
I have failed to build a house
artful quiet closed to none
where kind clocks smile at errors
mathematics makes of time
where the soil does not wash
women forget to be afraid
men forget the cold streams
of their children's unguessed minds

Make dark, my God, wreck
my walls and furrows! Let black
hover the marrow of my darlings
Prince? Poor man! You thought those leaves
were the banners of an exiled queen
with spotless hands, clear mind.

5.
Let loss let lack let stack
rake mow grain chaff
the last spectrum dust of us
Let the level mileward land
return the dust of handy eyes
harrow teeth rolled cuffs random straw
jay sparrow crow and star

Goodbye field stone river
Goodbye Legion Klan Baptist
Goodbye white virgin by willows
near a mudhole Goodbye Faulkner
Goodbye Elks and Eastern Star
Regulators Union deserters
Goodbye Davis Goodbye Lee
Goodbye evening yellow fireflies
mist of willow dancing ponies

Young father, who were you
Before your death, who were you?
Before you loved, who knew you?
Young mother, who were you
before your body burst and your
careful hands rescued my breath?
Young wife, who were you
before our child rotted in your
dear flesh, who were you?

God in the green of Heaven
imagined now, account to us
We are treated badly Pay us!
Give clods eyes Give us love
after good acts Give us back
wine for water knowing for seeing
Give us a law Lay the last straw
Give us full baskets to lay
at the base of the monument

Rack rifles Rack feathers Rack rue

BLACK BY WHITE

Alabama

to Martin Luther King

Come to the foot-killed grass, the rain-black shacks,
the porch rails solemn with flowers in rusted lard pails

Come to the varnished pine pulpits of ugly groaning churches,
to the beaten yards under China trees,
from cotton and sun on the blue bandannas of fieldhands,
their secret heads, their arm-frozen children like pineknots

and the crazy way of church singing, as if God were a hoarse frog
and hard times and broken bones were healed by a jazzy Jesus

And don't look lucky for being alive and hating white people
Come past the helmets and jowls of white troopers
your head bare to nightsticks   Walk your angry way,
drag an arrogant god to death between Selma and Montgomery,
die and be born—not on the road to Damascus

Free yourself from Christian violence and terror—
and from forgiving, the last white expectation and excuse
for little Sunday girls, so pretty! killed in Birmingham,
a *Bible* stolen by a servant in a white mansion
to teach a black man how to preach and pray whitely
O free yourself from gods that never lived!

Let your charity bloom only on the faces
of cane men and sorghum woman
no god ever helped or ever will
when they put bare feet to coffin end, are carried
in the hard song of a trumpet
to red clay no god has ever blessed

heard nigger to the last killed nigger,
said Sir too many times in dirty sorrow,
said God, as if that god had eyes and ears

For the Funeral of Malcolm X

> *As long as our civilization is essentially*
> *one of property, of fences, of exclusiveness,*
> *it will be mocked by delusions.*
> *Our riches will leave us sick. . .*
> —Emerson

Sellers, lovers of money, close your doors
On 125th Street bolt your shops
Merchants, count your money, and lock up
for a dead man who wouldn't turn tail
Collect no rent today from your slums
Kill no man in the names of your mothers
Take no payoffs from your numbered slaves
If one chair is sold, one lamp, one bed
they are broken on the floor of his house
If one wedding ring is sold, it denies
his love for wife and children

Are there any among you who know how it is
to live on slurs and sneers, chickenfoot, pigtail,
down to the last dime and the last bottle,
see the first cringe of a child at a rat's shadow,
with no place to go but to Hell and back?
Arc there ten men among you who can still feel?
and lock cash registers under racks of knives,
blues records and phosphorescent shirts

Don't trade his corpse away like a dead dog

    Malcolm dead in tabloid print
    New York newspapers gloat:
    A *Black* Muslim is dead
    A goat, a bony fish, not truly human
    He had a criminal record, they said

    American Blacks are free to kill each other
    or drop firebombs on brown Buddhists in Asia
    But they must not threaten white Christians
    in the Archdiocese of New York

Tonight blue lamps shine in Harlem
on the stone-cold violent avenues
in precincts of the sparrow and rat
Over his coffin a liturgy of silence
from beaten men and women in random jails
from Michigan to Georgia
All over Hell and gone

BLUES

*"I'll bet a bucket of shit
You will never fergit
Pensacola!"*
—Anonymous Navy Airman,
World War II

Bonaparte, Pass

Here   now   wherever
what is here   touching everywhere
all the now   here   and where?

archipelagos of islands

no man is a Donne
but merely Hemingway

"I could not pick the arrows from my side"

"Kipling stirs the blood," John Crowe Ransom said.

this is what it has come to
O let the dead bury!

huh-one   huh-two   huh-WAIT!
would Napoleon if
Sam made the pants too short?

phrase it?   possibly:
this code is for Josephine
this book is for Martha Gellhorn.

Humoresque

Dearest little Betty Maxson
I am on the train from Jackson-
ville to Richmond, Va., I love you

There were three long varnished boxes
with green wreaths and brass-bound corners
loaded on the West Coast Champion, too

We went walking through the park
goosing statues in the dark
Sherman's horse can take it, why can't you?

Passengers will please refrain
from flushing toilets while the train
is standing in the station, I love you.

Contrafunction Junction

Meet ya round the corner
in a half an hour
I just seen Pichel
in the music lounge
of the Fine Arts Building
sure   sure, sweetie
Pichel's here with me
hey   hey, sweetie
you should have seen Pichel
we got in the car
and he sat on the cottage cheese
he mashed it all over
then he dropped his cigarette
and set the seat on fire
then he spilled his beer
trying to put the fire out
sure   sure, sweetie
it's all right

just par for the course
if you know Pichel
you know old Pichel
meet ya round the corner
in half an hour.

Out and Anxious

(U.S. Narcotics Hospital variety show band)

Dad, *der du bist im Himmel*
O Dad, *der du bist im Himmel*
the fleecy whites are coming
to tear your still house down

Dear old Dad, the fleeces bloom without youuuu!

Dad, *der du bist im Himmel*
(at Georgia Tech they had Bobby Kimmel)
(at Mamma's house we had apple shtroodel)

By *mir bist du* who?

Central Park West

A fire-hatted Irish setter walks her
by a chain   escorts her nimbly
O I love her   love her couth mouth
eyes ears armpits crotch buttocks
nose teeth teats pelvis hands
because they're fragile

O bring her to me nightly, firehat setter
O I love her   love her puddly
fize punsks scratch clubbits cupcakes
with blueberries sourcream and bagels
fish and knishes, lox and sourcream
O how the overnight by Linda
with the vermouth and the onions
bagels lox sourcream and berries!

The End of Alice

The aurora was always boring Alice
she thought her vagina was a chalice
I say this entirely without malice
I could feel her midnight shun

rodless booty rodless beauty hardly
bawdy rootless body O
lawless booty jailbait maybe
beatific body O
Alice in her little Austin Healy
Alice sliding to and fro
I could feel her midnight shun

Tea growing in a Brooklyn window
I just heard my friend had died
tea growing in a private window
is she merely mortified?
tea growing in a midnight window
how can she be atrophied?
Alice, who went to and fro.

Perry Berry Been

Subtitle: Girl Carrying Newcastle

Mary Jo Berry loves her father, a lawyer,
and her mother, who was a Perry before
she married a Berry, and Wendell, her elder
Berry brother and John, her other brother,
and Markey, her younger sister. But Jack loves her.

Cheeseburger, With

Saw the coppery sore-armed fireman
throwing curveballs from the grave

while the Puerto Rican bastards
sold their mothers thirty ways

66

She's a red hot gristleburger
lying supine on her bun

and the totem pole is wobbling
on the North American.

Pussdido

(following Peewee's intro)

When to the sweet
when to the sweet
when to the sweet old sweet old sweet old
when to the sweet old sweet old sweetest
when to the sweet old sessions of

she lay high-thighed, cherubic
talking about it
no doubt about it, although
half-assed about it
maybe all the poor old sweet thing can do.

School Days

"Ahm a twisty twat from Agnes Scott
and I fuck for fifty cents."

Throw it to a tight
so firm   so tight
so young and muscular
a plume of black hair

I saw you standing there
in your Orlon, unaware
I asked the Lord in Heaven above
Is this sex or love?

(I was a Fundamentalist for the F.B.I.)

67

I knew a sorority girl
who exhorted her sisters
as they disbanded for weekend parties:
"Give 'em a tight screw, kids!"

O my sweetie's got curly hair
but I wouldn't dare
to tell you where.

Twee & Low

Stately geese   peahen ease
little sweet-butter-and-Danish girls
pimples and thighing waddles
Baby Ruths   Milky Ways
sucked in the movie show
beside an obese little boy

"Lean meat won't fry"

There was a boy
whose favorite candy bar
was Almond Joy

twee low · twee low
all fat girls shall rise
save youah Confederate money, honey
all fat girls shall rise!

Real Thing

(Sarah)

Th evening breeze
coalesced th trees
tenderly
I can't forget
charcoal briquet
hickory

who had   who had
my steakburger first?
tell me th worst
rain shine or snow
spam prem or treet
who stuck you so red?
who bled you that sad?

comingle
know
lost in the afterglow
how I could love you.

Virgin, a blues

She was married in a tapestry
and her Son descended and ascended
through the woolen trees

why is She weeping?
She feels her Son's body
in the basket of her body
descend and leave her empty
of no use further to the Father
Son and Holy Spirit
She is weeping
at His ascending and descending and ascending

see in the green forest
the feathery wrist on Her head
She in her sweetness
incomparable sweetness
O wood sorrel by the white wool river
chord her sugared bones!

first for the Fathering and Fathered God
second for the Son of the feathered God
third for the Ghost with the Feathery wrist
fourth for the Earth mother of men
Wife of the First Blessed of men
O thou Hand, thou Hand of fire
touch the Quaternity who sustain us
that we may drink the wine
and eat the hot-mouthed wheat
ground in the hollow bowl smoothed by her tears.

Greentree's Night Watcher

(June, softly as in)

To my wrists chain fast your criminal pulses
my dark night watcher
lock your hair, elegantly bright,
to my hands
your brown skin flay and anoint in the arbor
of my ribs caved for you each creation of the earth
and light that greens your turning body
stake your darkness to the close compass of my knowing

here all is meaningless night, meaningless day
do not hurry, night watcher
the light that gives you glory
will take it all away.

DEATH IN OREGON

The young trees are dry and light,
In the growing season no rain makes this land run green
Summer holds the gray odor of dying grass
The wind tacks dead twigs to fences
The branch of the willow tree is light
I lift it above the dark girl's head
She is light and dry
I am not burdened by her body riding my shoulders
Often her long hair falls in my eyes
Her black hair drowns the thin grass of this barren country
Light trees rise on my hands and let her go by
I hold a willow branch out of her eyes
Her eyes hold oceans that tilt her body riding my shoulders,
When she is angry her legs whip my ribs like the thin brown kelp
    I cracked on the beach
I remember the blacksnake whips of my boyhood when cruelty
    was the first lash of kindness
The girl riding my shoulders under the willows has a god
She prays her god to bless me,
She weeps often at night,
She is weightless, a benediction of sunlight on my body
The pale leaves of willow I lift let her dark head pass
Her ocean eyes tilt down to the unstable earth
Fish keep the curve of her lips
Her head looks down to this sparse earth
She weeps at night
She asks her god to bless me
All is perilous
Her god might not answer
She might not love me tomorrow
She may not remember the difference between loving a god
    and a man

Silently our skillful heads are helped go by the lightness
    of the young trees in my hands
I hold up branches out of her eyes
I feel into my ribs a small leaning woman whose face follows
    the earth at my feet
She asks her god to bless my journey
Her hair harbors me
I have carried her a long way
I have drunk light, eaten air, to carry her
How to make clear the soul I do not have—
    past or present, now or to be created—
is the walking I condemn myself to
The freedom to walk the past away by measuring nothing
    is the journey
I have carried her across America to this Western death
She lives in peril
I am careful
I hold trees away from her small face
She looks down to the dry earth at my next step
She knows she is safe where she is
She asks her god to bless me
I think her lips can wake up earthworms, turtles and carp
She puts small hands on my face
Her hair reaches down to my heart
She leans into the place where I took out my last rib
I hear her innocent confessions
I am a strange priest
My habit is her hair drawn over me
My altar is her elbow
The host I lift is a willow

UNDER A FLORIDA PALM

Stevens: "We say God & the imagination are one."
Hazel: "Imagination is one minus God."

Yes, Wallace, seas are splendid
Yet this is not Key West
Order died with you
Ideas, the very marrow of your carnal magnificence,
    are colorless
There are no cockatoos

A still lake near Orlando
    where a young widow coaxes hcr waddler over sand
    the boy puts feet into delighted water
    his head is a sweet melon crammed with seeds
    of the father he never saw or put infant arms to
    the widow stands thin in the white uniform of a nurse
    who draws spare blood from strangers

Grow dark, she is the pure profile of all orphans
    unloved, spun to sudden reverie in a nick of time
The dusk slant of her, Wallace, would remind you
    of a savage queen & the terrible pencil
    you hied a Cochin to
    that baton, that ordered change from
    delible beauty when she took her husband
    by the hair of his head
    in tight tumbled hilarity

to this green dark
this figurine embalmed
in my breast
not from Persia, Egypt or Key West

73

AN APPLE FOR JAN

Bright, O what quick eyes & voice
just the tip of talent, augur of the genuine
poet troubled by ice in the vein
Nervous as a snake she could make
songs on guitar yet so sad wander
hands weeping on strings into nightmare
Her night screams were silent
Only in day she taxed me for psychic rent

Block? No. A lovely American orphan
running where & when
drugs by the bale
abortion for birth control
Squirrely girl of Youth Culture
her totems: cock, rock & cocaine

Sunset on the Blue ridge where
I hear her voice My lost winced dear
how surely I care! I go to winter
weed crowns & harvest her absence
I bite an apple, sample it like her lip

When our bodies obeyed, how fine!

Iridescent entrails of cottontails
shine on a highway
as she tears my arms & guns
a little car away
Can I weep for more loss?

I could die of felonies not committed or why
I can say it was happy seed of mutant green before I
grew sorrow-cancer

74

By the fire she played guitar
for the neighbors & children
Then the ache of urgency

Though you have to go
Girl, sing for me

SUNDAY

"Is it five o'clock on the sun?"
—Wittgenstein

What is Out My Window

City of Churches   Sundown   October

Across the street a belfry holds warm pigeons
A tall stone house with green ivy and yellow marigolds
and a vacant lot beside a hospital,
a crabgrass short-cut for children
Two come across, one carrying his arm
over the other's shoulder,
in his left hand a softdrink bottle

Small girls in Mary's blue cross here
I cross myself, and smile

The belfry holds its signal iron
    over dented cars
In this house we are skilled workers
At night we discuss the tolerances of machines

The Way Here, and Here

Here I am schooled
Here I am paroled,
a boy led my mules,
in the distance pitchforks
and old hats, dogs barking
among wrecked automobiles

76

The time it took to arrive here
is the moment of seeing
morning barns and winter mud
where ewes were lambing
a dog eating a rabbit
in the rain,
trees with drooping shoulders

then Italian Renaissance houses
with cornices and pediments
scrolled in the iron evening
of streets without hoofprints

and houses of commerce
with carved names of the founders,
their hope of continuance
in photographs of daughters
in khaki riding habits,
sons in uniform, but always on leave

Here I am taught the manners
of rooms by day or week

In the university
Life Science is taught
and Human Behavior
But who will teach Death Science,
Luck and Chance?
the last light in an eye?
the afterlife of hair?

I make mirrors that keep faces
I tell hair
I collect the colors that scale from houses
I weave baskets like the veins of children and hearts
I want to be waxed and preserved
I want children like candles to illumine my breath

I have become a caller of telephones
with library ideas
There are so many houses!
with scheduled birds and sorrows
The frozen streets keep no footprints
How far from nothing to something?
From ice to sun again

The speed of dark is the same as the slow of light

cast on the statue of Lincoln
before the public library
near the used-car lot
by the skating arena
near insistent music

At five in the morning across the grave river
icy grass binds the ankles of mules
and the tombs of new people
and ricks of gray straw stand by the zero barns
Snow falls on the river, a moment white, then goes

My Union Card

Laborer, cousin, kinsman,
this for you:

journeyman carpenter, I leave you my hammer
    to nail pictures of nude whores
    on the walls of motels

house painter, cousin three years dead, I lay
    the brushes you gave me on your unmarked grave

posthole digger, take these gloves

truck driver, take my pills, whiskey and weary roadhouses

physicist, father, here are your tri-focal glasses
    behind which the light waves sound

78

gardener, mother, here are your bonnet and hoe
    for dandelion and plantain

pie baker, with your flower's name
    dead among your redbirds and spices,

we are wood by working wood
we are stone by lifting stone
we are air by breathing
we are simple and free as love
we are lonely and crippled as love
we are strong as love
we are orphaned to love

Some of us are dead now, some living among losses
May our love not be lost among my last voices

An Arrival

Through wired gladioli I hear music
I see my uncle's face in his casket
He had planted an early garden
His granddaughter sang for his funeral,
    her young voice drowned by the train
    that ran west towards St. Louis

That music was serious
    from the lips of a schoolgirl
    with fried onion rings on her breath

I can imagine music
What I can't imagine
is what I shall have to write
today for my uncle

A noun is the name of a person, place or thing
This is untrue
I know many untrue things
Therefore, by farmers in a baconed kitchen, I was chosen
    to write the obituary:

79

under a blue neon light my uncle lies
among mud-caked pigs, grain bins,
gladioli and dung, and a cowbell
wandering in the unincorporated town

The speed of the train to St. Louis
burns ragweeds between the crossties
Nobody can travel west from here unless a flagman
stands half a mile uptrack, waving

I wave there
Grammar?
Music?
I cannot hear

I Imitate Life

I walk down oak stairs in old houses
I walk up child-strewn streets
I wear a coat when the wind is cold
I recall how to smile in the houses of friends
I write many letters that I do not mail
I play cards, drink, throw black money
    on green tables as I lose
Loss is my skill

Let every man be perfect at something

Telegram

I have seen sidewalk mirrors condense my life like truth
Raining   Gray here
Rain   Gray   Night   Love   Stop
But love cannot stop
Trust you are well   Leaves colorful here this fall
The metal mirrors   I have sat in the automatic booth
and had my picture taken: four exposures for a quarter
hoping I might get a good one to send   Sorry they did
    not turn out   Will try again in near future   Love

The hair of the trees falls on my shoulders
Little rains fall on my shoulders
Eyes, too

Have not heard   Have not seen   Nothing to report
except the mirrors   Tried the photo machine again
today   Eyes not on the red arrows in the mirror
All wrong   Will try again soon   Love

Sometimes I wonder if you know
how the mirrors look at street-level

How can I tell you?
What holds honesty away?

I smell wet dogs
I smell alcohol
I smell the beautiful scent of your brain

The pictures came, wet and dim, out of the machine
Will not try again
I have been

An Absence

Knowledge fails   Touch fails   Vision fails   Love fails

Knowledge is no book against loss
Touch is no hand against loss
Vision is no eye against loss
Love is no sacrament against loss

I close my books   I fold my hands   I close my eyes
    I fold my loves

Valentine

Too many kinsmen asked me to say our sorrows

Those who sat in shawls near coal stoves under small American
    flags and photographs of sons at war

Those who filled glass dishes with rock candy
    for no mouths
Those who listened in varnished parlors to piano music
Those who played electric guitars
Those who shot themselves in the feet in Italy
Those who said I love you without meaning I or love or you
Those who lay with ears full of blood and sun in Africa,
    unspent postage in their fatigues

and my cousin, whose submarine delivered him to tearing fish

What Do I Know?

What is my knowledge? Parents I can't find?
Brothers I visit once a year?   A sister who
is a Pauline Christian?   A wife anointed by pain?
And a child who was taken away?

What shall I say
of the many beautiful
I name equal and beautiful?
They are changing
They are always changing
What is my knowledge?
To say my love, with awe

I Greet Myself Near the Beginning

I know nothing but love, a thing
    of grass and brain and hands, open

I know nothing but love, a thing
    of schoolrooms and chalk and reading

I know nothing but love, a gallery
    of photographs of dead children

I know nothing but love, a wallet
    that identifies me past recalling

I Greet You, City

I did not ask if I could be
Many times I have regretted that I became
But there is no escape from knowing   And
I knew always in this place I would happen

I am your house painter and cement finisher
I have worked here these ways
I tell your time on the dials of my eyes
I have bled dark residence, City

My shadow crosses your spires at noon
My shadow crosses your taverns at midnight
Your streets breathe me in

Sister, Pray for Me

Sister, your white headband, your black dress, your unread lips,
    your steel-rimmed glasses,
your short pointless journeys into my colorful and dying world,
    your cold beads, your delicate chains!
Not that we have stopped on the street where I pass you
    each day, or spoken

We know many things that are not spoken

O,stranger in Christ, what have you given up?
What have I embraced?

Sister, in your dear Christ's only name, pray forgiveness
    for your tolerable chains and my intolerable freedom!

Adoration

My life is a cathedral
My life bends in chronic adoration
My life is stained green by copper flashing
My life is supported by flying limestones
My life crosses itself, and stares

Beautiful child, while pigeons murmur, tell me
the woman ways of your quick radiance!

Mondays we begin all over

The street is littered with music programs
    where they have fallen

I lead with hands   Who follows?
I cannot look back   Who might be where?

Army stores wrap me in wool
Across the street pigeons nestle
    under a churchbell

If I sit in a deaf room with blind walls this Sunday,
awed by the slow morning radiance,
who can say no, if I say yes?

LINES IN PRAISE OF MYSELF

My passion, drawn from me, bitter and rich

My gall in an era of chronic humility

My candor that stares in grief at my country
   while a pious Texan makes war on small nations

My refusal of false gods while others write essays
   and plays about saints

My laughter at Mary, my mother, my wife
   while Paul prefers abortions to condoms

My simple denial of the lies of my parents
   while others build self-abasing psychologies

                     ***

My love of children and candles while
   churchmen set up No Trespassing signs

My favor of poor while government offers
   dollars for pride

My awe of rivers and columns of stone,
   the visions of builders:
   David, Cyrus, Jefferson, Mao

                     ***

My incontinence to the celibates

My land-drift to grit-city

Nothing saves honor but to be
   assassin of lies

LETTER TO THE KENTUCKIAN

to Wendell Berry

1.
My earth announced by rising flocks of leaves
Under green a horse's veins strut on his running
Sunflowers bend east   Their tongues take summer's host
In the morning mist apple buds flare like candles

Here comes the sun to my magnet!   Too much life!
I have bitten my mouth   I spit blood

In my mouth more than thirst for my own blood and the blood
    of other animals,
the holy mass of summer! yes
and I pray by waving a scythe at high grass

In one long rush of my breath
a dandelion's white head
bursts to tufted life

Fly, little wild birds!   Handsome cock fathers, sing!

At the end of cut weeds and battered clods
    the kiss of water
    stigmata of sun-fired windows
    echo of walls
    silence of photographs
    patience of drowsing flowers

Fireflies light their day   Cells settle   Sugar seeps
I hear the scrolls of corn stop unwinding
    and the birds stop reading them,
    tuck head under wing

I have my own twiggy dreams—
To town where carnival birds
   fly on whistling sticks

Weave a circle round me

I'm dizzy   I'm lucky   I'm magic!

And I can step in any river twice

2.
Your hard hurt bring me   your unread books your wrong
eye-glasses your illegible letters your relief checks used car
payments your hard hurt hearts bring me   your death insurance
bring me faceless documents printed in code dealt you for inked X's
and usury   your hard hurt times bring me   your bruised hands
porkfed weakness green vomited mornings your lardassed lovelings
bring me your dry faces dry gardens dry batter your dull senses
your hick brains your helpless hands your slat backs having bent
over your already done work bring me your grinning brown tobacco
mouths your loud laughter you fools! you fools before bankers and
sheriffs O weak weak and hurt hard by your dires hurt blue and
so sadly go inferior clumping into general stores go rummaging
in black back pockets for dimes among bent nails and twine go
let the townsmen take the dangling buttons off your Sunday coats
pluck lint from the chains of old slow watches and other
poor white and black bone and metal cold now in their
candied town hands

3.
Crossing the Ohio
where my homeland breaks at the river
to an orchard of tombstones
beside the superhighway
where engines sing in anger
under a neon frieze
of hamburger and beer stands
I have come to gentle you, Old Ones
to soothe you like colts with my hands
carry whispers like wheat to your corpses

Old Ones, honor me now
Your bones decorate my wrists
Dead children swindle my arms
In the exile of recall
From the hourglass full of spiders
return me your sweet hearts

Yes, Mother, your pulse sobs
over a hip-carried child
Father, your serious eyes!
Yes, look me straight in the face

Dead blood turns black
Grief is a way to turn
But who can see tears in the rain?
I gaze at your flowers of lime
I call these stones by your names

4.
White scales the house   The painter is dead
Green binds the house   The trimmer is dead
Hands search the house   The lovers are dead

5.
A gone world, ours   Once upon a time

Our chronic dirt, hick curiosity, boys' blood,
our hands cut to the quick
bled like the sawed-off horns of cattle
from sharp tools our fathers thrust into our ribs
before we were old enough to shave

Learning was pain
during the first terror and failure
But what elation to discover
we could pinch, pry, jimmy, jack
a world into place!

After we knew sunsets
fierce as the severed head of a horse,
washed the crusted blood from our foreheads,
took pleasure no longer in killing,
learned how to smile at wives and children
and nod our willing heads to hairy sod
dream smooth dreams,
not shouting fear and rage,
learned not to attack the already wounded,
but kiss eyes, hair, faces of sufferers
and care for all suddenly young and torn

What meaning now?   Virtues?
Repeat Colonial tales of common acts and faith?
Green people, green rivers?
Devoted builders, defiant to kings for sake of us,
bringing fire to our hearths?

Who, if we shouted, would hear us in the Drive-in theater?
We have seen used-car bumpers welded into sculpture

THE HUNTER, THE CATCH

We go from swelter to freeze
My woman strikes to fix green
    fires that cringe
Our son holds a hatchet that cuts
    blood, if I let
Cold mornings I kiss his belly
I kiss his mother's eyes

Raw, after that:
Run upon drunk hill boys
    who promise to kill me
    if they catch me out again
I show my woman how
    to fire the .410
Her Indian eyes don't blink
    at the full-choke lightning

No deer today
Sundown blinds snow
Fire in my house
Oak smoke climbs to the North Star
I lean to the window's hard light
    where two loves wait me
    with hands the same size

I track down the woman's tongue
My neck wears her gold medallion
    stamped with a fertile stork
She presents her son as a gift
I load him on my neck
Her delight is we run and kiss
She wants me to find her
    hidden in rowdy black hair
She lifts me on fine-honed legs
Her teeth grin like rain

I'm earth-spawn
I belong to pine

My body their rainbow,
wife & son will cry
my knocked box down

MARRIAGE SONG

To the light white spring bloom falling over the dumb
pages of winter-turned books and simple signs of hands
consecrated by a man and woman walking under spring rain,
   cousins to minnows and wet calves

their pulpits formed in religious rocks
and surrounded by cattle, wet noses down—
the color of hair, the smell of melting snow
and to rusted mouths, soon as winter wears out mud
into unfolding apples and cicadas, sunlight on sudden tongue!
the blindness of, the strength of spliced arms
carries grain and salt to young muzzles,
lets go the regaling fire of tufts, sprouts, perilous buds,
going free the green awful shine

FOR RIA, CHRISTMAS, 1975

If I try tobacco & corn harvest with sore arms
   from a house where a woman & boy stray & steam
Take in love for berry eyes & mahogany legs,
   candy canes, wear & tear of child bones

I'm coaxed into a year of grains' yearn
   & sullen humility under the sun
Gloved in wife & child blowing lung-frost
I cut green hickory to sing
   on the hearth

Promised infinite lucky Spring
I tune my carcass
My young son crows
My wife swings & shines
I dive down my heart's run
   & drown in their sweet spit

A RITUAL

The Dead Stars

The language of harvest was sugar, having
    no intervals, no melodies,
perfect for insects and the steady airs
    they carve;
they forget to sting, to breed;
the ardent air is time made visible
among the white branches of apple trees;

being natural, you understood that world's
    terrors
and invented intervals of song to avoid
    the drone of too-small wings,
but you could not escape selection and death;

August was a mirage of black starlings
that roosted thin irises of glass,
the stuffed owl's eyes above the lintel,
scaled feet rooted in the watery light,
    a twilight of buckled wings;
you thought of distasteful grubs in tree bark
    and of barbaric invasions;
you saw a bird drop, bounce on the mast,
    roll a dry inch;
lice abandoned its body and began the long climb
up the tree where blood is unfaded and sweet;
below, still quills beckon a putrid breeze;
while you watched, thinking: Cherries!
earth sieved thin reddest water
    from a drying beak
and, among apple cores, little pigs found
    your fabled star.

The Meadow

My girl lay in the sun;
that burden was too loud;
she took pennies from her knotted kerchief
and laid them on her eyes

though she was not dead
or thought of herself perishing
until she left the sun and was cool
    and could forget
the hot astonishment of the coins;

a tigerish bee dandled from the stem
    of a white clover,
white silence mounted by an orange sound,
water drinking an ingot of the sun;

a cloud swam past the sun's cornice;
a tree spilled petals down the inverted sky;
a tailtwisting wind mouthed the petals,
cream for my girl, sprouting breasts, to drink,
for my young girl to rub on her knowing face,
my child to curd with praise her wishbone's meat.

The Scolding

Archangel of summerside,
the woman threw a beaded shawl on her head and came
waving a finger, preaching to the ground,
a farmer's wife, unafraid of sailors
who fed black cats the heads of pearly fish;

blue tattoos on the red-brown arms
gave her wrath grace
against the feeding of shipboard cats and raccoons;

my girl, high in the twigs of the mast, silent,
pictured the dustless parlor, the piano,
the pared fruit wax-like in glass jars in the cellar,
blue milk in crocks on the porch, the wooden horse
she rode by lamplight to keep warm;

95

then the stench of hot bananas, tarantulas
   drowned in leaves,
the water verminous and scrawled with oil
moved those dominions of her skirt
towards darkness where the rib of summer caves,
sails bursting; the surly waterspouts
in their plummet grow long sighs of wrath's
   grim zodiac;

my young girl's pennants mourn
bailing cans full of sailors poured at her feet,
the carcass of the world sprinkled with lime
against swellings and the yawn of ribald cats;
drifted in powder and lilac water,
my girl looks from the dark tent of age-sweetened flesh
   like sick girls' dreams.

The Corpse

Your branchy bones had not yet hardened,
   your sea-gills dried;
you cannot suck and spit and screw your head
   like an owl;
you cannot walk;
you cannot pick up scissors with your hands
   to cut out cardboard sailors;
you cannot speak;

your head may as well have been a blue balloon
   with eyes, nose, mouth painted on;
it floated away, light with mystery;

but these are only signs of a headstone's rout;
I take for dimples time's smite on stone.

The Hill

You lie under the hill
and love conceals you fearfully;
you who wore my ring
lie under the hill
and love, a deaf musician,
stares at your beadless silence;
you lie under the hill
and love disdains a hovering
of starlings on telegraph wires
at their punctual distances;
your straight hair undertaken,
you lie under the hill
and love stops ticking;

for you the ticking stopped
like melting icicles;
for you the humming cold wires
do not signal
across your lucid winter;

for the poverty of your dear love,
for whom love is dazzled by—
silence, radiance, doldrum of candle
light on window-hosted snow are all.

SMALL RAIN

Child, under grass, always at night
your close cries and falls of clear hair
lock me with love; my bare fields rove;
my locked love under grass cries
and falls always in your deep hair at night;
my roving fields lock you here round my love
in the burst green of trees where my nailed eyes hold
their crosses up in a stray rain to catch your water face
here in our broken knowing, in my ransom hours
    of rain standing
always at the green falls of night grass
above my near love, roving towards the broken horizon
in its rainy hearse that carries me lost in the fall
    of bare horizons
round our green sad morning marriage, beautiful child!

May the brown faces of broken clay
that hold anxious flowers on sudden clear graves
above rusted wire frames and green twisted ribbons,
left helter-skelter beside the brave hearse,
reflect your greenest hopes against this cold new time
    of slow leaves curling
and the haphazard faces of flowers that mock
the careful movements of your unlucky thumbs.

O broken child, cut free of our eyeless children, O love!
suffer your beauty; suffer the greed of green to kill
    at the ends of your weeping hands.

CELEBRATION ABOVE SUMMER

Hear dark the priestly insects of my endless summer
    coast down to cells of wax,
and kind weeds bend my flowers to their colors' end;
in my thin acres hear time burn stones deaf
and radium's fine ticking to my flaunted ironweeds' blooms
stop in amazement at rough measures, twined of handclasps
and the rule of hammer-bruised thumb;

                          wonder and stature
of young celebrations shot from the dark earth build silent
my endless prism of rusted axes and fruit jars glowing with fireflies;
and curled in the quiet speculation of clods, my black calf,
sweet and voluminous, hooves maggoty in stiff air, columns high
the buzzards sailing;
                        O see my land turn back,
· my summer ponds waved with cattle, my ironweed candelabra
    burning,
my knotted chickens, sure claws austerely clamped and
    dawn-triggered
to sweet August branches, sap-crested, wild and immune;
O hear my crony leaves measure fine spaces, inviting
    the brisk moon-stares
to shout out clear recks under green flies, beautiful calf!
your magnificence sickens me with love;

see my slat gates nailed back to the green yawn
    of grass; see, under sour water,
mosaics of mint, and my country run
back everywhere green, green.

99

A REVEL

Black trees ice-barked and flaming shake braids of hair
thick with evening odors of soft coal over my bemused house,
hush down the white walls and nut floors and pepper-ripe sills,

hold my cistern-sized and perishable earth still until rabbits
    scream above and moles run under orchards of snow
and my chronic harvest stores little false deaths, the fertile
    comedies of all saviors' third mornings
when under ice tomb-wrecking seeds wake and storm sunwards
    their green legends,
hold clear stars in purlieus of adventure, glitter in the fern-kept
    history of my trees and as peacefully burn and die,
where rabbit scuts burst white in the black hickories
and the gamecocks' shanks grow electric in snow, thin-stamened,
the pale round signatures of combs and hackles new sunflowers'
    gazes turn;

        here in a funnel of leaves the white roof water carves
brittle wreaths incensed at the candors of dawn
in early resonances ascending of gold green shanks budding
    with spurs;

immersion of morning here gives back sense to my swift creatures
that as quickly die as corn tassels and blood-burst rabbits
    curled in sleet;

        O empty birds, cry in the matted heads of my trees;
acclaim my deaf gullies with your little tongues! charm
at dawn the quickening woman in my house riotous with eggyolks;
rake your harsh thighs; be always keen for cutting;
fly in the perfection of your injuries;
while my landed hand throws pale grain upon snow,
preen the bleak land you tow your exulting tongues over;
walk lightly on nests that lie in blushes of straw, full;

100

the woman in my house is beautiful
because she can turn herself into a tree or a mother or a slut;
I think of the grave delight of being mirrored in her eyes
    deep as honey jars,
haughty and sorrowful because she knows she will as soon die
    and her borrowed ribs sieve minerals quietly;

here between ever reweaving root latitudes, anther and filament
prize her wholly mortal and heavily scented and young,
going by sun and season,
to whom my drunken ponds wave breathless violences.

SLEEP IN AUGUST

Where veined rocks pulse in the sun's aftermath
the dry air moves across the earth;
leaves tick the visible days
here in time's motionless always;
among slow-burning stones in the quiet rise
of leaves, on their green frieze,
only the hooves know August's iron dances
in a flow of light over sleek bodies and wire fences
that will hang up, to bleed and clot,
in nibbling thaw and pelt-slipping rot,
crippled dogs and foxes
at the loose ends of cold chases;

in the hot yards the men's and women's hazy
faces and the honeyed children's crazy
voices swarm under a ceiling of fire;
the chained fields and nailed-down houses hear
the axe in chaste trees as they tear
and fall with a dark smear
of green against sunset, in the wasp hum
and kerosene smell of August;

sheep doze in horror of maggots in the locust
groves, and the fields mold their stones
into elemental forms,
self-contained and open and free from the incantation
of this delirious season
that runs riot in my veins, turns me to stone;

high in the trees dark birds dream
the clay of silence into presences
like tragic frogs; in the hollow sky
dead stars arrange themselves like men and animals going by
slanted in myths; then if, stopped by no watches,
I lie down on thin grain
do not wake me with promises of green.

102

SUMMERTIME

At daybreak the other
men & I gather
We throw hay over
the shoulder
At noon we make over
the children & eat & drink beer
& check the bailer

At night we pour water
all over our skin & lie down
Then terror
an Austrian doctor
said would be there
is there

A BOUQUET FOR THREE BITCHES

EMM

Wedding March

1.

Start with little
Grow warm as your woman & child fill

Dig the soil & show your small boy
where his hands drop seeds
Glee when they rise to light
green as flies

Praise the sun in March
Delight in metals, file hoes, whet knives
for calves & peaches

Put two pillows under

After food & water, find art
Calendar of a funeral parlor
where a friend lies pasted

Less is best
It makes want sweet

Test time
Circle the days of agony
when your woman fucked in Virginia
while you lay ill

Calendars tell Easter's white gloves
& a child's eyes lifted in sunrays

Grow cold as gizzards
Hardwood wormed
Tongue sour
Spiders in pillows

I see her licked legs & gored vulva
With our son's red crayon I mark the calendar

Time is only distance from love

It's cold under the poles where I hung the deer to bleed
Sunflowers gray & empty as I

Beat the feather pillows
Step on spiders as they run

Time the clock, the calendar, Roman?
Let piss climb the wind

Son, your cold fingers
curled round an acorn!

We are frozen earth, my son, we are snow

Suffice in drink
Scare a nightmare

Go to the funeral home
See your cemented friend
Wear a necktie below your breath

Drink & cry

Who is as far away as I?

2.
And he took his hands and garnered my wife's hair
and he pressed his belly against my wife's little round mound
And he stuck out his tongue and shot it into my wife's mouth
and my wife took his cock in her hand
and guided it into her pussy
And he moved my wife's beautiful body
And she craved as she moved as he squirted

105

on the body of her son
on the hair of her husband
flooding her young son's navel
greasing her husband's sick veins
with semen groaned from her lover

When I breathe it's my death
When I weep it's my funeral

3.
Under locust trees a brother beat to death
    his brother with a crowbar
Here a brother shot his sister to death
    after their father's funeral
Her drunk passed-out head was
    the groundhog in his riflescope

Here are rusty machines
A young man just out of prison throws bales of hay
    for a case of beer
Boys play cocks like flutes
    while my wife fucks another man
Wet moss, wild lilies over
    a wife who slides slick as an eel
I'm blue to the gills

I see you walk to him, as to me
Arms gather bodies into, as if me
You kiss & whisper, as if to me
Hair, bone & blind thighs wallow
Bitch & dog! Sow & boarhog!
Crayfish are cleaner in their slime

Leave my drunk silence drunk smile drunk loam
drunk car rides on wine runs drunk walking
on my mountain drunk onion pulling
Leave me
drunk & loving
   my arms in rainy thistles
   laughing at pain a long June
   harvest of my joy

Here's a broken fence
An empty posthole
Lawn overgrown
An owl in the apple

Fruit, rot
Weeds, take grass
Posthole, cave
Fence, fall

JTR

Her boast was she was
the consummate cocksucker
in Washington, D.C.
High on drugs she went down on
jewelers, short-order cooks
car thieves, musicians
fancy dude cocaine dealers

But she never learned
how to kiss mouths
She thinks she's a great lay
but is not because she closes
her eyes and is only dreamily
masturbated in isolation
and stunted greed for
what is not ever

Her fury to males is so
strong that in copulating she
got pregnant three times

Her excuse is that fucking
takes two and protection
is as much the male's as
hers so her revenge is to be
knocked up and bear
all anxiety and pain
for male brutality, or
what did she expect
except venereal scabs?
This is her way of turning things
upside down and inside out
gouging out her womb like
any slave She does not know
this is ethical suicide

Before we wed she boasted
she had fucked mostly married
men—she doesn't know
whose sperm lodged the last
two times—I asked her
please to stop praising
because I happened to love
and why be assured your wife
has taken into her body
every pus-filled prick in D.C.
and Alexandria especially
left so frightened and hateful

"I could fuck for cocaine tonight,"
she said. We were in D.C.
where she left me to return
to her loveless scene:
a line of cocks
as on a butchers block
drumming her snow-numb tongue.

FB

1.

And now the death of my life I have lived bounds
in low lightning, still trees surrendering bud-breath
& I've become the fireflies' delight, winking my own cold eyes
all night when early June mates them & my lost woman
can't stay the little hill of my lone haven, but is God-bait
in death-trap, her terror in all my hungering since the wool cap
of my childhood   I'll not blame a horse, a dog, a rat
for having life   I've fed many, never myself & loom
over great cities as Wolfe-led I sense her swift internal terrors
& polyglot rot in tons of semen shot per second in New York City
& ewes torn in Jersey & I returned to acres where the earth is not
picked & scabbed over with asphalt & cement & only in time
to be left here like a post that can't even wave goodbye or grow
in the loam of that woman's arms before hunger, pain, rain

2.

I walk towards my death like a new friend, hoping
to love her, free of tabus, for death is my mother
& the daughter I'd mate with   Who could love me to make up
for having no lover alive, in this earth, more than my death-bitch
with familiar breath & limber tongue? Fran is her name
Still & now, sweet heart, when you draw black rhinestones
Harbor unified, Black Sun excellent, I steal fire
& burrow this light into you
this know to know
how all your tears run to my trust
And care all my stamens & go   Tell the vines flow
to the roof of my mouth!   Give me one sweet time
& I'll stay your evil till the sun stares me down

3.

There was City & a City woman   Christ, one up & two down
Night sudden woman, show me my bitter eaten
leaves, gray me to the savage mouths of insects, free
my solid arms of hold & ravaged lorn time when I swam
in quarry water derelict & passionate in umbilical scent, went
a braided boy of birthday all alone, no one

to comfort me, toned to my body to stay me this new day of my birth
raining on tongues of brown thrushes in cherries & me
Locked twigs held blest blue on a voice charmed into time
saying vows of telephone love, I alone in the perfidy
of her blue chatter
I hear Bags & Trane   Christ, two up & one down
Can you, woman? Dogs of my rusty blood bark Come on,
sweet swatch of hair in my teeth, swarth, fine!
Let all sway & weed go down to bloom Nothing I say makes
    gauds grow
or tell true & stuck woman to tell my rue to
Bless her, her tired body, Bless her sucked breasts, her god-in-me
Take her in tow   There is no tarry
the clods & toads away
This is my face blistered with lime in country time
The white rose, yes

4.
For perfidy & betrayal of my rainbowed love
under awed trees
for denial of my careful hand on her face
& the god-gone wonder
What do I wish for the destroyer of my crowing faith?

May she have a brief life
may she die alone without comfort of friends
as she condemned me to loneliness
may she have cancer of the cervix
& be childless by tall boys who will enter
as she killed my son
may she die, not in pain, like country folk
but slide down a cesspool of pills
like New York copouts usually do
& I'll not even learn if the bitch lives or dies
My ears are full of tobacco

5.
I've taken down the pictures
Her image can't hang in this red house
to shadow my grim life-spring
& the turnips I say grow & sing to
for this is the fall of the crosses of weeds

As I lean towards my death, Mother
What is a kiss?

DELLA YOUNG TO THE POET

Well I was glad and happy when the mail came
I been wanting to write you a few words
but couldn't find your address That's my failing
never know what I do with anything
and put in hours searching and studying
But I have got so I like it Something to do
I set up till 1:00 a.m. till after midnight
I wrote a batch of letters Now you wonder
One to Bud and wife's boy in Germany
one to Bud and wife in California
married with four boys one in Germany
and another in Vietnam one retarded
and the least one still at home
One to Madonna that lives in Indianapolis
Madonna has one boy through high school
and a sick husband in the hospital
I must not forget her She and her husband
send me money all the time
for medicine and things to eat
I am not keeping roomers anymore
I pay the whole shebang lights water telephone
and all breakdowns like sewer stopped up
painting and papering The light system
went out Something wrong and cost $40.00
had to pay that but Madonna and husband paid half
We have had two deaths in the last two weeks
Luther got burned up in his own house That ain't
no way to do things I wished I could have told
poor Luther that ahead of time and saved the funeral
expenses Allen the funeral director got his new
funeral home finished it off with a green awning
just in time for Luther to burn up before his time

The first funeral was held It was a double deal
from the Legion and the Old Soldiers
Luther and a old man that stayed all night with him
years ago when they worked on the railroad
and ate beans from the same old black bucket
We have a new preacher Bro. Davis from Arkansas
He his wife and two little boys They come
up to me before Church began and talked to me
and made the little boys talk and call me Grandma
When they went away all around me
them little washed-up devils says who
Who was that old woman Sister Young?
I was that sister Young I said the new preacher family
they said they didn't know which one and I said Who?
I am who prayed here before you knew who
I was that old woman that knew Bill Hazel
and went out to pull the weeds off his grave
and I am who nursed Bill's boy Herbert when he was sick
and I am who took Bobby Hazel, Herbert's son, in hand
and taught him verses and spelling before you whoever
you are ever got up here to this country
so don't go asking me I felt ashamed for them
I said to them Well, if you want to get acquainted with somebody
write them a letter like I did
I had wrote the preacher and his wife soon as they come
They didn't even know I had a daughter named Madonna
Well Madonna's man's doctor said can't go much farther longer
He has diabetes Boils come out all over his body
Neither is Madonna She has ulcers Had all teeth pulled
$400.00 to get them out Don't know how many stitches
in the jaw But she got new glasses and can see again
I get choking spells sometimes Sometimes when it's bad
I don't even recognize Ed when the police call me to come
up there and take him out drunk Sometimes
when I think about it I take choking spells Sometimes
don't even know my own little brother Ed in the jail
Eddie is all the brother I have now He is very poorly
He has took to drink Eddie with his heart condition
He and his wife was drinking and she got mad at him
and broke his guitar that he had won the Nashville contest

113

with He shake his head He just cave in Eddie and was so mad
at her She broke his guitar right over her knee and throwed
the pieces against the wall She said Go get em and pluck em
one more damn time And shake his head and look at his prize
guitar like a batch of kindling for the fire
so finely He said all right I am leaving
I will just move out to the hen house
She said Good enough So he took some old clothes
and a skillet and some flour and a coffee pot
got him an old broke chair and set in the hen house two hours
it was getting dark the kids come a yelling in
and somebody knocked on the back door It was Ed
Said Can I borrow a little baking powder?
She shut the door in his face and laughed till she cried
the kids cried half scared and slinging snot
This is February 2nd and the groundhog seen his shadow
but I ain't worried about it It's cold with a deep snow
5 degrees below zero All water pipes froze
I have went to Services at Church every time
They had to slide me in the car with a shoe horn
All around me six widow women in a block of me
One old she-devil hard of hearing I can't talk to
That old deaf widow has a little fice dog named FDR
She watches the Television Can you beat that!
Hard times here The faucets all froze up
but I pray daily I wish you and all of yours
health happiness and God's Grace
This botched-up letter is like Bill Hazel used to say
Looks like somebody had written it hisself!
I love you all, all my dear kin and never saw any
of our tribe but what hadn't the same right to their name
Hard times here after all was gone, the girls, my husband
sick or dead or moved down to Florida or to California
But Bobby you didn't never forget to come and visit me
when you was in this part of the country
You come by and sat on the porch with me and jollied me
and reminded me when you was painting Luther's house
before Luther burned hisself up in the fire
how I had carried you up a gallon bucket of ice water.

114

DEATH OF THE FARM WOMAN

Same bones, same face, same hair
I touch now, after the embalmer

lying level body, tame to the dumb frame
of the metal trestle

Railway crossings and bus intersections
where you waved sons away, old woman

Went to bright town, pinched timid dimes
To cheap cafeterias we traveled, thought them rich

But our gardens, the fruit of!
sat paring apples after sundown

said for saying, word for word
in country, Mother of dandelions

How we ran! where the water found us, with me under your heart,
young startled girl, waiting for my eyes to open

Not any clod any weed any dry furrow any spraying weed
or clod's crumble, not any stick of wood wears your hand again

So easy, to lift you now on my eyes
as the sun changes

lift you above bronze handles of your casket, above plastic grass
to a green place, on your own dumb sayso

As you stay still here, breathless
in the presence of cedar,

clay to my clay,
your meadow arms hold silence to our stillest leaves

your love-dried lips, brought up with wax, do not say
You sew these ending stitches through my lips

CAROLINA

Leave Taking

I am kissed away by sober women, those saltless good women
Goodbye to the air-conditioned car that carries Mother & Sister
   in white Sunday hats and gloves
    south to Florida,
riding thigh to thigh in the ambulance of optimism

When you go away, Mother, Sister,
in your long desolate car with radio loud and trunk full
   of beans, corn and Bibles,
Alone here, I study minnows and toads prettier than words
The creeks ask me silence to hear in
   below the thunder of moles
My arms are wet with our Father-Husband's ferns
My cup spills over with leaves
I train them up the trellis of my windpipe
I laugh their browning edges green again!
I whistle back to our dear dead Father's birds
   here on this hill

Noon of goodbye, and where? The engine of a tractor
   mowing far away sings hornet songs

To My Loved Woman

First wind of fall tonight, a fire in the hearth,
my father's stuffed birds on the mantel, rain, hail,
then a sky so cruelly clear that the North Star rang like iron
I curse nothing, not even the wasps that sting me
I look, I listen, I love

116

I rattle with unstrung nerves freely with dying weeds
My arbor is swollen with grapes that will slowly ripen
Each evening I walk out to see their gradual blue
I sit on my mountain under a full sky
I am empty of hate, free of illusion
Real deaths stare back at me, not just the imaginary
deaths of gods that breed religion and philosophy
I hear the loud teeth of a dog, ripping
first the brown hair then the thin blue hide of a groundhog,
now the chill gnaw of gristle, loud in the human hall
I have cut through that meat and was stopped at the bone
Destruction, the squander of continents, the gunning down,
in Asian meadows and American cities, of brown men and women
Blood is the crown of my race   How good of my father
to have killed only himself! He kept Christ's thorn

Wanwood Leafmeal Lie

The mist drops slowly, Father, falling in
The wood is ricked, maple and oak, in dry
Your birds sing heavily this fall, your sunflowers in
In the night mist heavy animals go   They sink in
The earth under the grape arbor is rich
as your caving face
and the frail bones of your hands, yellowing in
Potatoes and onions sweat your cellar in sweet
But the grapes, Father, the heavy clusters gather!
much happier than a Christmas tree   O, Father, you
lying therein, you rotting too   Dear Man,
I have cleaned our hoes and rakes and hung them in
to dry   I have told you our happiness
and why   Father, I am willing to die

117

HEADS UP

to Kenneth

Heads up to sight us, peach and honeysuckle swells
all over the twigs and rails,
corn grains in the teeth of loping rats
And us quick children in a summer of carbuncles,
all us rough cuts with berries blue
and blood on our mouths that call and call
    to the udders of German women

And at fall's last burning, gone small into wide snow,
    stalking a cedar, sneering at ice
We pissed on the same cold stone
And you, Little Boy, inside your far far fire
wore frost on your face like a beard

You knew as a child there's no mercy for poor

Grown sharp in our carnival minds, the axe at Christ's Mass,
the cedar so mute in its own scented crying
stood ceiling high, blistered with popcorn and red
    paper chains held by wheat-glue in our poor

Brother-man of our chained blood-brood of fond spawn
I have come to know blood when it dangers the State:
the cinders of Sunday black girls in a Birmingham church,
the corpses of white girls whose fear-wet flesh was a threat
    to the National Guard of Ohio:
(Malraux recalls that a holy man once came to Gandhi and said,
    "The gods are dying. Why?"
    "Because the gods can live only while they are beautiful.")
O, brother dear, our gods lie faceless and quailed in cured blood
    in a country of no surprises
We have felt the visible blood leap from your broken mouth
    and my slashed forehead
pumped from us rough-cut horseshits, American ruffians
    who fucked the strange strangers and cupped our mean hands
    when the Eagle shit

118

And now in your face broken to kindness I see
smiles and caresses for all your tame darlings,
my own face now wreathing in this time of love
after wild and cruel sang away
and scars dimmed from red to blue

O, the years, years while the angel grew
on our Christmas tree!

And here it comes again like rain on Indiana,
on our way to an old barn waved with high hay
we stalked our impervious poor

And in the water of our dear father's grave,
    all his wet walking
sunk in a small mound of sand in Florida
And our dear mother wreathed in the wet of her
    grandchildren's kisses
Ah, her waning hands! O, say yes!
Brother-son, take my hand and say yes

For the poor, love grows round and fat on water

I nailed up a photograph of our parents standing
    in blind wedding clothes
before a small house circled by fodder
    and hens pecking rocks for craw grit

At home, home I lean beside a tree

They could not save our rainbows

Child rain knows there's no mercy

If I honey your hurts?

I've been stopped here some nights
I don't think the days are equal
This is a far cry
I sorrow into crops of nails, herds of stars, rains to the East run
My wrists ring with love's pulse
Is love legal tender?

Down in me, still rejoicing for our brutal innocence, still

There is this little I keep in trouble
That you shall know
That you may be
Only that you go

SHENANDOAH

Before I began I had all there is
Now I don't know where
I go & smell like a wet shot
I call myself & preen
I know how long it takes meat to rot
I crave & don't spare

I'm what my father whipped with whips
I'm what my mother wept for keeps
I'm my brother's nails
because I eat with my fingers
in front of his blue-eyed children
Sister suffers me for kindness

If a man thought he was understood
he's a fool & should suffer
If he thought he was loved
the flash came quick & I wasn't there long
in Shenandoah's soft dale
The sad girl with wise eyes—
how dense was her body when it found its way?
Lie out, still   Surround grass in blue city fists
and long swayback hunger!
I pool in her nerves, swig & shine
Yes is the muscle of the blind flower
Yes opens the mouth of the dreamer
Yes is tart & suck of laughter
I woke & saw cold light
on the tight sills of her skin
under the vines of blue hills, red apples
O, the cunning leaves, the chill grapes!
I see why Jackson
rode round the Union

I sway here   It's my time.
I stay anyplace over
The courthouse clock in Winchester
told my crimes to the Greyhound riders
I looked around but saw no blood
I'm blind as a sitting duck
I came here in a bad sleep
I bought up my arms for salvage
in the junkyard of Roanoke

I wanted to tell about
but got sidetracked
I'm what anyone would call
when I remember my given name

In the rack of a cattle truck
calves scratch my hands with little tongues
I make my own music
I catch a hatful of whispers like old rain
that will not fall as long as I

WIND FROM NEW ENGLAND

I'll not have rats
I keep snakes
The well is clear

I go by the rule
of sticks & stones
I live on the edge
Down can't matter
Scars grin at the sun

I'm here, hide & hair
among watery roots that wave
their white entrails
single & slim

All here green as fire
I'm in the place where snakes
leave their scrolls
Before day can break
I wave the sun up
& call the birds here
to festoon our sunflowers

I lean on a fence
evening while white stones fly
over the pines, then the moon
tracking wind down
New England Freeway
Taconic & New York Thruway
Sawmill River Parkway
past November granite
your sleek hearse
ribboned with ice
& you in the iron ground
eyes melted that spelled my name

Pretty snakes lie by the fire
under your crucifix
The water is clear
There are no rats at the door
where I shouldered you up
like a sack of potatoes

GREEN GIRL

to Antonia

Come, Little Leaves

Hill high as the sun colors day
swarms of cold gold leaves blind me
    and sweet oak smoke
The stems of meadows' torn weeds fume

What will down will down
    from the seed crown

Beside me a green girl says, Don't cut it,
    that weed wants itself
Her eyes know happy happy! I'll not kill

For her sake I take off my gloves in any cold
Her body is the only ruler
    I imagined as a boy I could measure things by
Her ears are my music
Her tongue is my spit & speech
Her ankles tie my bouquet

Beauty isn't said
Beauty is tried like lard from the carcass of a pig

I see them, all my things riching and rotting
how I know them today & will become
Now in revelled October their colors are drawn

But to see her my her, her gladness to touch
    in a wild field
is to be myself warmest all at once
and tuck her smiling knees in my hands
And she is all bunched up and happier than a squirrel
    with alerter eyes
Little leaves parachute to her hands

125

Under the Meadow

In the frost night clear as the scent of cloves
little heads cry ice and curl down like my cold own
They have more petals to confess yes to
They are more beautiful than I, even in my own rooted say-so
Yet I, too, nod my head to my own brown season
    and lie down in a drift of thin waned leaves
I crumble, too

While the green girl takes my frown away
and brings back all the slaked rages I wore out to scar
and I see a little sight and I fix the star of myself
for her wherever she has in wonder gone

I'm here to find her visiting punk and roots and late shoots
    by the water
My forehead crosses her into light's late comedown
Come full dark shine, we'll learn how to crawl
    where the peaches buried their coals' magics

Magic—I have a claim on some, some

All things alive are the same tame
Death is the broken eye and the brain's small rain

My loveling goes ways by this falling stream
O, shudder, grass shelter!
Wind, make room
Hush, bush
Don't catch her breath
Don't take the blame
Wave my sweet heart on

Ode to Autumn

Fire of sumac, and the green running
Still days shine like copper
The bright white night grass leans
    over gravestones like lain down lambs

The dog I dragged dead away
    has caved in to fangs and bone—
    no buzzards, no rain
    Pure sun carved him

Into this leaf gulf the burnt and burning stars
call fire and tall weeds burn their crowns
like girls under kisses and hands

Girl, give me samples
My bed smells like apples

Here in a turmoil of sweet willing swill
mad bees suck mud
Pear-fisted children grin and run
at their blossom ends

A cold wind blows in
Soon my grapes will tease foxes

The cricket and I are alive because we make noises
I pretend Indiana didn't cripple my poor head
I walk under a moth's quick kiss
    and bats cheer me with a loud clapping
    this cold evening

Late light rings the axe of my father
Dark settles the gentle flowers of my mother
And what light for my own Hell-coming?
Sedges, I drew your short straw
My inferiority makes me cry
down a tin gulley of yellow school buses,
a boy who hoped for little more
that a clear idea of his cold Harm-coming
And what for my singing?
The hungry birds look down, and are fed

I've not been false since yesterday
I tell a lie only once a day
   and that to myself
The leaves shudder at my truthfulness
Marigolds greet me and bring their friends
We talk yellow

I'm not going anyplace
except to throw lime on my lost dog
I'm swayed like a wheathead to loving and wishing
   for light
Rotting hide tears me
Peeled fangs, onions, hay I throw
I bend under litle broken bushes

The owl is full of shrill spittle
The crayfish bubble slime
Stars whine a far far light
I throw bottles from a fast car
I call and catch fire
My sorrow plays, Here comes,
   ready to die, or not!

Now in brutal October
Keats, Wolfe, Thomas, move over
I'll drive this time
Detroit Iron, don't stall
While white maggots swim
through the pine gloom
haul my loveling home

And If I See Her

And if I see her in any picturing of blue eyelid
hanged lip or any felt slippery go to hip or ribsense
brown breasts or any smelled go to thick swollen hair
or gummy blue eyelids or her rain-sodden heart, felt
little sudden pump of now and then and then again, sucking gore
and full felt woman nosing my neck or she lay at night
afraid unless nose bled breath on me or she shaded my country
ear and gander neck in a morass of rotten cotton breath
running alive with love's worms
And if I hear her in better frost air walking by my side
or at midnight's crow and ecstasy where her low voice came
I stammer you, my love, you with my love's surprises, yes
and guess how much I stammer you into my only haved haven,
my love, and one white cat I wish on you to nap at your feet I wish
you for a funny trick or why cat and I roll over for you with your
    promise
of food even though our god fell down the sun in a tree out the
    window
and after your bent tracks lost sight night after goodnight
And when I taste the hare-like sweat of her body spined down
and olive forehead and the salt of her tears and turned aside
to the carcass of a dog deepening under high wheels of buzzards
over my meadow and yes then into my mouth the thin liquid of her
terrible tongue
For there was a swarm of bees in the belly of the dead dog
And smell her tears, the girl's weeping, kiss her trouble,
dearest daughter of my shot heart, bad head, my last living loving
and all ferment of our short goings and comings

And if I feel her body uprooted in my arms,
my hands lift, my lungs breathe into her drowning and save

Eyeless in Indiana

I saw them fall full, the tree over the leaf,
   the well over the water, the girl over the cloth
I let my head fall back full in joy
My bones genuflected to her spine
I gave her an apple smile for her cider,
   for her joined and jointed body
   like a petal puzzle
   all yellow as tobacco

See my marbles, my slingshot, my bike
See an old radio that ladled the syrup
of the Hit Parade into frosty spireas
   beyond the yard fence
See my Indiana
Central Dream of this continent
It's called "Stardust"

The Harley big bike rides dead Dean
The Big O dribbles a ball at Crispus Attucks
Here are the slaughterhouses of Armour and Swift
Petillo, 1935—Andretti, 1969

Let them rev, let them speed to the circus
smell of blood, castor oil in carburetors
to sullen thwarts that die men down in bottles
and the slow rot of exhausted joys

These men crawl like maggots on my once-beautiful eyes

Here are my hands
Where are the pillars?

Night Bloom

Horses tear grass near my door
Stars are so mute where they are
Stiller yet in this rotting rail forest
    my father's black tongue whistles
    his birds down at night stir

What leaves grin there!

My heart brambles the mud of my lonely body
    where only creek buds blame and care

After the high-maned corn-crazed heads go rough and cold
    of milky colts sucking while walking
    and fragile hocks dance
I go back into holy laurel
I weep at the sight of a girl's shoes in my pine house
I hear her say senseless sounds in the pitch of her love

I obey bloom in a bad head
I have made more mistakes than God

Signature

A lost dog sings and marches at night all night
    over my sinking head, my dark sunflower
He walks my cold night out. He cries and weeps
    in the stumps of dead trees
He sounds my name in the stillness of my hiding
And startled out of meat-dreams strays among hungry thorns
He sings in the absence of human voices
    and walks his nails across me whether wither these leaves
    and flooded wails to the dark hollows of my hooded hills

My head is what rides under the trees
My arm is what strikes the soil with love
My legs ask dew my next step
My mouth curls a voice to this shape
My name hides now and is hidden

O lift my head back gently and lay it down